CHÂTEAU

A Taste of the

Cook, Craft, Grow.

DICK & ANGEL STRAWBRIDGE

A Taste of the CHÂTEAU

Cook, Craft, Grow.

DICK & ANGEL STRAWBRIDGE

SEVEN DIALS

First published in Great Britain in 2024
by Seven Dials, an imprint of
The Orion Publishing Group Ltd
Carmelite House,
50 Victoria Embankment
London EC4Y 0DZ

An Hachette UK Company

1 3 5 7 9 10 8 6 4 2

A CIP catalogue record for this book is
available from the British Library.

ISBN (Hardback) 978 1 3996 0319 5
ISBN (eBook) 978 1 3996 0320 1

Typeset by Anita Mangan
Printed in Italy

www.orionbooks.co.uk

Contents

Introduction - Welcome!

Welcome to A Taste of the Château, a journey into the heart of our home and a celebration of life's simplest pleasures. Nestled in beautiful rural France, Château-de-la Motte Husson is our forever home and a source of inspiration with its vibrant, continually changing flora and fauna. Every season brings its own magic, its own flavours, smells and reasons to celebrate.

These pages have been crafted with as much love and care as our Château's restoration and are a visual record of a year at our home. In our world, family is the cornerstone of every festivity, every trip to the garden, every bloom that is plucked, and every craft made. We had so much fun talking about what we would like to include, and we hope this true enjoyment shines through. Just in case you haven't worked this out yet, when you see writing in bold, that's me, Angel, telling a story.

And when it looks like this, that's me, Dick. Join us, as we share our cherished recipes, including family favourites, family hand-me-downs and new ones inspired by our travels. Our recipes are more than just instructions; they are stories of seasons and love, words that are meant to be savoured as much as the dishes themselves.

Our gardening tips spring from the soil of practical experience and are imbued with the joy of watching things grow slowly through the year. From sowing your first seeds to harvesting your bounteous crops, we'll share stories that bring the outdoors to life, and we hope we will get you in the mood to get your green fingers dirty so you can use some incredible home-grown produce in your cooking.

With so much love in every celebration we host, they deserve to be showcased in style. Our crafting, intertwined with the laughter of our children, echoes the spirit of old and new.

Whether it's my seasonal table decorations or home-made gifts for that personal touch, making crafts with your own style and character will add charm to every gathering and remind you that the journey of creating is as important as the final product.

Each chapter of this book is a passage through times of the year that hold a special place at the Château. From the crisp whispers of spring, through to the abundant harvests of summer, to the golden glow of autumn and the whispering silences of winter; every season is a reason to gather, create, and taste the bounty of the land.

That's why we decided that the flow of the book should not only be seasonal but would use our own family calendar of celebrations as touchstones for your inspiration to host your own. These aren't prescriptive, of course, but we hope will give you a glimpse of how we curate our own events.

A Taste of the Château is more than a book to us; it is an invitation to weave the joy of these moments into your own life. To find beauty in the petals of a flower, warmth in a home-cooked meal, and laughter in the creation of something handcrafted. It is an encouragement to pause, breathe, and relish the joy of being together.

Step into the Château with us, where every day is a discovery, and every night a celebration and thanks for what we have, even if that just means taking ten minutes to sit by the front door with a cup of tea to reflect on the day. We hope there is some magic on these pages that inspires you to create, to grow, to cook, and to cherish the moments of joy that build the mosaic of family life. Here's to discovering the taste of the Château, wherever you may be.

A Family Update

What a difference a decade makes!

Our Château dream has become a reality, and we find ourselves waking and smiling as life here is all that we hoped it would be. Arthur and Dorothy are growing up so quickly Angel and I have to remind each other to savour every moment. It feels like it was only yesterday that we first entered the Château with Arthur toddling along holding our hands and Dorothy in a papoose attached to mummy's hip, yet nearly ten years have passed, and here we are with two bright, lively and fun to be with children who are growing up way too fast.

What a decade it has been! When we turned the corner and saw the Château for the first time, we had no idea what adventures would lay ahead for us, and now looking back through old photos or catching a repeat of Escape to the Château just reminds us that so much has changed! Our children are always the best

indicator of this, but the Château has evolved beyond anything we could ever have imagined. We continue to look forward and feel that we are entering a new era with our family and the Château. We moved to France to be the navigators of our destiny and 'smell the roses', and after a lot of hard work, it's really time to put that saying to the test.

We always try to live life to the full, and so take every opportunity to create memories, be it sitting down to breakfast together, pottering in the garden, or enjoying an evening with friends. We hope this book encourages you to do the same, and to use the words of Kipling from his poem If, let's all 'fill the unforgiving minute with sixty seconds' worth of distance run.'

Enjoy the book and thank you for your support and love.

Love Angel & Dick

A Taste of Spring

I n the northern hemisphere spring starts with the equinox, around 21 March, and is always a time for optimism and reawakening. The sap starts to rise towards the end of winter and, as with all things to do with nature, we tend to have to be responsive rather than in charge. Geoffrey B. Charlesworth got it right when he said, 'Spring makes its own statement, so loud and clear that the gardener seems to be only one of the instruments, not the composer.'

The first wild daffodil, the first primrose, the air starting to warm . . . If you are lucky, the sun will shine and for the first time that year you can leave your jacket in the house. Spring brings a lightness and a different bounce to life's rhythm. While I love snuggling in the winter months, when the first signs of spring appear, I want to open the window and tell the world! The first family walk in spring is always rather special and seeing the first cherry blossom makes everyone's heart sing. There is nothing more beautiful than the delicate, tiny, pink flowers of cherry blossom. Our walk often starts by the trampoline and goes all the way around the moat. The trees are bursting with buds, there are pops of yellow and purple appearing in the wild meadow and there is a sense of what is to come. Dick is always excited to see his walled garden coming back to life.

The start of spring is not necessarily a clear demarcation between the bad weather of winter and the warmth of the new season. It seems that sometimes March doesn't always 'come in like a lion and out like a lamb', and severe frosts can continue well into April. If you're planting out, you have to be vigilant, as it is not unusual for it to be a tad chilly, but the colours of freshly emerging buds show so many variations of green it is breathtaking, and by mid-season

everywhere is vibrant and new. If you are producing your own food, there is a period of the year called 'The Hungry Gap', usually a few weeks in April and May. It's the hardest time of year for UK producers, as it comes after the winter crops have ended and before the new season's plantings are ready to harvest, so while spring is exciting, we must remember it's a time for preparation and planning.

Easter allows us to enjoy everything this gorgeous season has to offer. The dates always seem to take us by surprise (did you know Easter can vary on a recurring sequence of nineteen dates ranging from 21 March to 18 April?). For us, Easter is a real family affair. It's often the first time of the year that we have lamb and it's also the moment when I start to get crafty with the children again (after a hugely indulgent and crafty December). We also make time for the annual spring clean, which is secretly one of my favourite pastimes. It's all hands on deck, because after many months of celebrating with family and friends, the Château needs to get ready for guests again.

Our event season starts in May, so while Angela leads the spring clean, I'm outside taming the weeds and ensuring the garden is ready to be productive. We spend a lot of time outside together as a family, and even though Arthur will often try to sneak off and dig a hole, everyone plays their part in getting the garden prepared. In the past, I've given the children their own beds to take care of and that's been a real winner and a great way to keep them engaged! We love to come together for May Day celebrations, which have their origins in the Roman festival of Flora (the goddess of fruit and flowers) to mark the beginning of summer.

I often think that the spring months can be just as warm as summer. Maybe it's because we have just emerged from the harsh weather of winter, but it's a joyous time to be together outside. The colours, the wildflowers – it's all to be celebrated! Whether that's pressing flowers, adding a bunch of wild daffodils to your dining table, or sharing seasonal food with your loved ones – whatever you do, it's sure to put a smile on your face and a spring in your step!

Contents

Easter Celebration

Recipes

Crafts

May Celebration

Recipes

Crafts

Getting started in the garden

I f you have a garden that you want to make productive, or even an area you feel could turn into a garden, it helps to know where to start and what skills you need. There is a school of thought that you should observe your garden for a year before you even think of starting, but we haven't got the patience for that. Although, I'll admit it is worth taking a look at what's growing well already; my advice would be to start small rather than commit to too much.

Sitting down and planning your garden is a great starting point. Like a lot of tasks, the preparation often takes the most effort, but it's worth it to get it right. For example, if you can plan to have your rows of fruit or vegetables aligned north to south, each plant will get the best opportunity to absorb its share of sunshine as the sun passes across the sky. Once you have a plan, it's time to get into the garden to do your weeding, digging and general tidying. It's only then that we allow ourselves the pleasure of starting to sow and plant. Read on for more suggestions about what grows well in each season. I would caution you to think carefully when you buy your seeds. If you have loved your crop, you can 'seed save' in the autumn and grow the next generation the following year (see further notes in the Autumn section), but this is only possible if you have bought non-hybrid seeds.

If you have not got as much preparation done as you would wish, consider covering the areas you have yet to cultivate with cardboard, black plastic, or old rugs or carpets, to cut out the light and stop anything from growing. The lack of light will make weeding much easier when you return to it.

Many new gardeners see wildlife as the enemy, and it's true that there are insects and larvae that will eat your plants, birds that may eat your fruit and mice that will nibble your pea and bean seeds. However, let's not forget that wildlife can be useful in the garden, too. We try to encourage birds that eat garden pests, such as slugs, snails, aphids and caterpillars, as well as pollinators, like bees and butterflies, and even frogs, toads and hedgehogs.

The season's first edibles

There are some things you simply have to grow in your garden. It may seem a bit underwhelming, but a row of radishes is a must. Why? Well, there are lots of varieties of radish and they are amazingly quick growing. You can see the first leaves after just a couple of days and will be eating your first radishes in as little as three weeks. They benefit from succession planting, so every three or four weeks we plant more to ensure we have a plentiful supply of fresh tender young radishes. If you find you have too many to eat, there is always the opportunity to let them go to seed and collect the seeds for sprouting.

Another 'must plant' are tomatoes. Home-grown tomatoes taste like a tomato should, and they can be transplanted to grow outside so you don't necessarily need a greenhouse. Don't be scared of trying the heritage varieties, too, as they look and taste

really special. Growing your own tomatoes allows you to enjoy the benefits of fresh, nutritious produce that is rich in vitamin C, potassium and fibre, and the lycopene in tomatoes is a powerful antioxidant, which helps protect against heart disease, cancer and other chronic diseases. To grow tomatoes successfully you will need a rich fertile compost or soil, and they thrive in sunny, sheltered spots. They need regular watering and do well if fed once the plants start to flower. Choose a variety that best suits you: determinate are the bushy plants that work best in pots or hanging baskets; indeterminate (or cordon types) grow tall and need to be supported.

Peas and mangetout are a no brainer and they are an amazing snack in the garden.

Arthur and Dorothy don't think twice about wandering around the garden to see what is ready. No surprises that the strawberries and soft fruits are the number one target, but they are followed very quickly by the peas. Peas can be planted under cover in late winter, then planted out every couple of weeks until early summer. When planting under cover, we use waste lengths of plastic guttering and drill holes in them for drainage. We'll sow the peas in a staggered formation and, when they are big enough and the risk of frost has passed, it is really easy to slide them off the guttering and into a pre-prepared trench. To stop peas from becoming slug food, make sure you support them with pea sticks to keep them off the ground (any twigs or small branches from the garden will work for this).

In France, they appear to have a love affair with haricot beans and I have found it hard to get tall varieties of runner beans to train up wigwams and trellis for the 3D element I love in the beds. That said, I did find the climbers eventually and now have a supply of seeds. As a little aside, I love the fact that it doesn't matter what way you plant beans, the shoot will always grow up away from gravity to push out into the light (negative geotropism) and the root will always grow down into the soil.

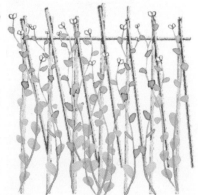

Herbs for now and the rest of the year

When you plant herbs, you want them to be useful straightaway and remain so for the rest of the year. The most important thing is to plant them somewhere convenient, so you can access the herbs when you need them. We grow basil on the windowsill and in beds in the walled garden, but nine times out of ten, it's the small pot in the kitchen that we use. Most of the commonly used culinary herbs can be grown in gardens, beds, raised beds or containers. We tend to consider our herbs in two categories: perennials that we know will be there when we need them; and annuals to be planted throughout the season.

Let's consider perennials first. There are two decisions to make – which herbs do you want and how many of each do you need. Here is a list of what we love to have available:

Bay

My sister Glenda gave my father a bay tree before she died, and my father gave a cutting to my sister Pamela, who gave a cutting to us when we moved to France. Our tree is now flourishing in the walled garden. It loves well-drained soil in the sun or part shade. Leaves are best picked in the summer for drying.

Chives

This is the easiest and most forgiving herb to grow, as it can survive in almost any soil. Cut the stems down to the ground after flowering to produce fresh leaves.

Rosemary

As well as having fragrant leaves available all year round, rosemary produces nectar-rich flowers for bees in spring. We have hedges of rosemary so we can use branches on our barbeques to smoke the meat. It is easy to take cuttings and propagate them.

Basil

I had always failed to keep supermarket parsley alive, so when I first met Angela, I could not believe the pots on her windowsill. The answer: completely over water them! It worked, although I couldn't bring myself to do it. I use the parsley technique to re-plant the basil pots and, even though I was always taught not to water basil in the evening as 'it doesn't like going to bed with its feet wet', I allow Angela to water it at will . . .

Thyme

We seldom cook mushrooms without butter, thyme, garlic and crème fraîche, so we have bunches of thyme in lots of little areas. To keep it bushy, you need to trim it after flowering.

Now for the annuals – we tend to start these in the greenhouse, then transfer them outside mid-May when the soil has warmed up.

Parsley

A must-have herb, but it takes a very long time to germinate (up to six weeks), so we have been known to buy organic plants from the supermarket. We soak the pot and tease the plants out before putting them in a much larger pot of compost that we also soak well. With a little care, within a couple of weeks, you have a number of plants that can be spread out to provide lots of parsley.

Call me old fashioned, but I never saw flat-leaf parsley when I was growing up and I prefer growing the curly variety; it just seems to be easier to chop.

Coriander

We always have coriander growing through the warmer months. We grow it mainly for leaves and sow small batches every month or so. This succession planting ensures we have a continual supply from mid-summer to early autumn. As it is an annual, coriander will do its utmost to set its seed and die. We embrace that and collect the seeds for cooking and growing the next year.

Mint

As well as having many culinary uses, mint is also one of the best herbs for attracting beneficial insects to the garden, such as hoverflies, lacewings, bees and butterflies. It loves to spread, so we plant it in old, oversized plant pots, sitting just proud of the level of the earth, with the bottoms cut out so the roots can go down but not sideways. The plant will need to be divided regularly.

Wild garlic and strawberries

In April we are still waiting for the new season's produce in the garden, so nature helps us out. Wild garlic grows in abundance in late March but we missed having lots available at the Château, so we re-planted some in a bed in the walled garden and in our damp woodland area, and it is sure to spread and become prolific. Young wild garlic is great in salads, wilted as a veg, added to a buttery mash, or used to enliven soups. It also makes a terrific pesto. Look out for it wherever you find bluebells, as that's the environment in which it usually thrives.

St George's mushrooms are another wonderful spring bounty. They taste delicious! I always remember St George's day is 23 April, as it's around that time that they mysteriously emerge. Before we turned the area in front of the Orangery into a wild flower meadow and the grass was much shorter, we were delighted to find a ring of mushrooms there in the third week of April.

Growing strawberries is incredibly rewarding. We usually get our first strawberries in May and they are worth waiting for. Home-grown strawberries will be the best you ever taste. (Once you've had your own, eaten in season, you'll find it

hard to buy a supermarket punnet in December . . . just saying!) Year by year, your crop can increase manyfold if you choose to propagate the shoots (the plantlets). It is worth noting, though, that the plants should be replaced every three years, and it is best to move your strawberry beds to avoid disease.

In our first growing season, we bought about a dozen strawberry plants and, if I were to guess, I reckon we now have over 200. We have a wall in the walled garden that has wild strawberries on it and another near the moat. We do not tend it in any way, but every year the plants produce a handful of highly perfumed, tiny fruits that we

savour. Last year, Arthur was fascinated by a white Japanese strawberry, so we bought a single, rather expensive plant and this season we have a full bed of white strawberry plants.

Top tips for growing your strawberries:

- Weed the ground well. (You can put down weed suppressing membrane and plant your plants though it in April. This will keep the moisture in and reduce weeding. If we use membrane, we spread straw on the membrane to stop it being so ugly and we also use straw on earth beds to hold in moisture and keep the fruit off the damp ground.)

- Plant them about 40cm (16 inches) apart.

- Plant them in full sun for a sweeter fruit.

- Don't forget strawberries also thrive in containers or hanging baskets – don't forget to water them!

Our Perfect Spring Breakfast – Eggs à la Château

SERVES 4

Chargrilled asparagus fresh from the garden, poached eggs and a dollop of extremely rich hollandaise sauce – what could be more perfect?

Ingredients

2 bundles of asparagus stalks, trimmed

200g (7oz) butter

4 whole eggs, plus 4 yolks

4 tsp lemon juice

Methodology

1. Place a griddle pan over a high heat to get hot. Add the asparagus in batches and cook for 5–6 minutes until lightly charred and al dente. Remove from the heat and keep warm.

2. Bring a saucepan of water to a simmer (for the poached eggs). Meanwhile, heat the butter in a small pan over a very low heat until the milk solids start to bubble. Remove from the heat.

3. Place the 4 egg yolks, lemon juice and a pinch of salt and white pepper into a blender (or small food processor) and blend well. Very gradually pour the hot butter into the blender through the funnel with the blade running. The egg yolks will initially heat up with the butter and, as the temperature increases, they will turn into a warm hollandaise.

4. Once all the butter is added and the sauce is thickened, poach the whole eggs in the pan of simmering water for 2–3 minutes.

5. Divide the asparagus between 4 warmed plates, top each one with a poached egg and top with the sauce.

Easter Celebration

Spring Vegetable Soup

SERVES
6

This is a sweet, buttery broth full of the colours of spring vegetables. You could also serve this thick soup as a vegetable side dish with chicken roulade or poached fish.

Ingredients

100g (3½oz) butter

8 baby carrots

4 baby parsnips

8 small shallots, peeled but kept whole

1 small bulb of fennel, trimmed and cut into 8 wedges

4 garlic cloves, peeled but kept whole

800ml (1½ pints) chicken stock

100g (3½oz) frozen peas or fresh mangetout

500g (1lb 2oz) buttery potato purée (made by passing your buttery mashed potatoes through a sieve), to serve (optional)

Methodology

1. Melt the butter in a large saucepan over a low heat. Add the carrots and parsnips and cook gently for 10 minutes. Add the shallots and cook for 5 minutes. Stir in the fennel and garlic and fry for a further 5 minutes. Shake the pan from time to time so the vegetables brown evenly.

2. Pour the stock into the pan and simmer for 10 minutes until the vegetables are cooked through.

3. Add the peas or mangetout and season.

4. To serve, divide the vegetables and broth between soup plates and, if wished, pipe some potato purée onto one side of each bowl. This is a lovely, light spring lunch.

Wild Flower Salad

When picking wild salad leaves and flowers, pick them in moderation and don't pick any where they may have been treated with pesticides or peed upon . . . There are lots to choose from including:

- Nasturtium flowers and leaves, which are peppery.

- Dandelion – the whole thing is edible. The flowers need to be picked young and have a honey flavour. They get bitter as they get older.

- Wild bergamot flowers have a sweet, minty, spicy citrus taste.

- Violas/pansies look amazing and have a grassy flavour.

- Tulip petals taste like lettuce with a peppery aftertaste.

- Lilacs vary in flavour from nothing to 'lilacy'.

- Rose – we make rose petal and honey sandwiches. Chose the most fragrant but remove the white bit at the bottom of the petal as it can be very bitter.

Ingredients

a handful of mixed young salad leaves per person

a handful of edible flowers per person

FOR THE DRESSING

5 ripe strawberries, hulled

50ml (2fl oz) orange juice

50ml (2fl oz) basil oil

1 tbsp caster sugar

Methodology

1. To make the dressing, press the strawberries through a sieve into a jar or bowl, then whisk in the orange juice, basil oil and sugar, and season to taste with salt and pepper.

2. Make sure the leaves and flowers are free of dirt and wash them gently, if necessary. Place the leaves in a large bowl or on a large platter. Drizzle with the dressing and arrange the flowers on top to look lovely. Serve at once.

Easter Egg Basket

France takes Easter very seriously and every year there is an Easter egg hunt in our village. It's delightful, well organised and a great way to spend the morning! Whether you're hunting in your garden or at a more organised affair, these little bucket liners are a brilliant addition. They can be as easy or as difficult as you fancy and will last for years.

You will need

- Pencil
- A small basket or bucket
- Tape measure
- Fabric (you won't need more than a metre, but it depends on the size of your basket; scraps are great to use here)
- Scissors
- Sewing machine
- Cotton thread
- Needle
- 2 pieces of cord or ribbon the length of the circumference of your basket
- Pins

Instructions

1. Measure the circumference of your basket or bucket at its widest part and add 4cm (1½ inches).

2. Measure the height of your basket or bucket and add 10cm (4 inches).

3. Cut a rectangle of fabric to meet these measurements.

4. Cut the fabric in half.

5. Place the 2 pieces of fabric on top of each other, right sides together.

6. Using a sewing machine, sew a 1cm (⅓ inch) seam up both short edges, stopping 10cm (4 inches) before the top.

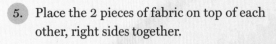
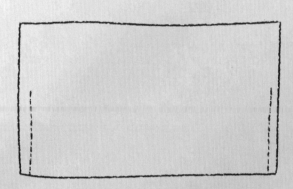

7. Open up the sewn seams and fold back the raw edges. Where the two pieces of fabric haven't been sewn together – the 10cm (4 inches) section at the top. Hand stitch the raw edges to the fabric, to create a neat edge.

8. Measure 2 pieces of cord or ribbon to fit the circumference of the bucket plus enough to tie a bow.

9. Fold the top edge of fabric over the cord, creating a 5cm (2 inch) channel. Sew this with a 1cm (⅓ inch) seam to enclose the cord.

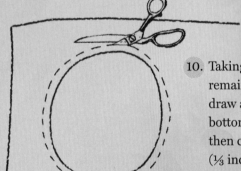

10. Taking some of the remaining fabric, draw around the bottom of the bucket, then cut a circle 1cm (⅓ inch) bigger than the drawn line.

Top Tips

Don't sew through the cord!

11. Pin the circle to the bottom of the sewn fabric liner (by putting the raw edges together), making sure the right sides are together. Once it has been pinned, sew together using your machine with a 1cm (⅓ inch) seam.

12. Turn the fabric the right way round, and put the liner inside the basket or bucket and fold the top of the liner down.

13. Use the cord to tie in place around the handles and gather to fit.

Decorating the Easter Basket

You will need

- White felt (I love to buy a pack of felt that has a variety of choice and colour)
- Scissors
- Glue gun and glue sticks
- Cotton thread
- Buttons for eyes
- Tiny piece of black felt
- Black wool or embroidery cotton
- Big-eyed needle

How to

1. Cut 2 sets of bunny ears out of the white felt (template included), i.e. there will be 4 pieces of felt.

2. Put 2 felt ears together and sew around the ears to join them, leaving the base open, then repeat with the second pair. Turn both ears inside out, so the stitches are on the inside.

3. Sew or glue the ears in place on the front of the basket or bucket liner.

4. Glue on 2 buttons for eyes on to the liner.

5. Cut a small elongated triangle out of the black felt for the nose and glue in place under the eyes.

6. Use the black wool or embroidery cotton to make a mouth and whiskers. Stick on with glue.

Important: have fun!

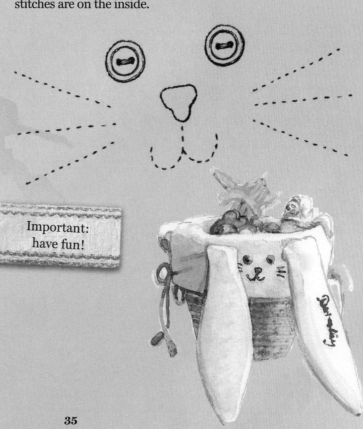

35

Clams with Parsley Butter

SERVES
4

These make a great starter or would be good as a sharing dish placed in the centre of the table for people to graze on . . .

Ingredients

40 good-sized clams (we use Palourde, which we collect from the Brittany coast)

100g (3½oz) butter, softened

4 tbsp chopped fresh parsley

1 garlic clove, crushed

200ml (7fl oz) white wine or dry cider

Methodology

1. Wash the clams in cold water to remove any sand on the shells.

2. Place the butter, parsley and garlic in a bowl or mortar and pound to a paste. Season to taste. Form the paste into a sausage shape and wrap in clingfilm. Chill until required.

3. Place a large saucepan over a high heat until hot, then add the wine or cider, which will steam and sizzle. Immediately add the clams, cover with a lid and shake the pan. Cook for 2 minutes, shake the pan well and cook for a further 2 minutes. Take the pan off the heat – the clams will have opened but will still be soft. Set aside until the shells are cool enough to handle.

4. Split the clams and keep the half of the shell with the clam in it, discarding the other. Arrange the clams in their shells on a tray (or snail platters, if you have them, as they are perfect).

5. Preheat the grill to high.

6. Thinly slice the herb paste and add a slice to each clam. Place under the grill. Cook for 1–2 minutes until the butter bubbles and starts to brown. Serve warm.

Cheese Soufflé

The thought of a soufflé scares lots of people but it tastes great. This needs to be accompanied by a green salad with a sharp dressing and fresh baguette.

Ingredients

65g (2⅓oz) butter

4 tbsp freshly grated Parmesan

50g (1¾oz) plain flour

300ml (½ pint) milk

100g (3½oz) grated hard cheese, such as Cheddar or Gruyère

½ tsp mustard powder (optional)

½ tsp Worcestershire sauce (optional)

4 medium eggs, separated

Caution

The cheese has to be strong as the egg whites will dilute the flavour – we love a mix of strong cheese and finely diced smoked trout.

Don't be tempted to look in the oven while it's cooking!

Methodology

1. Preheat the oven to 210°C/Fan 190°C/410°F and place a baking tray on the middle shelf, making sure there is some head room.

2. Melt 15g (½oz) of the butter and use it to grease an 850ml (1½-pint) soufflé dish or 6 × 150ml (5fl oz) individual ramekin dishes. Dust the insides with the Parmesan, shaking out any excess. This will help the soufflés to rise.

3. Melt the remaining butter in a saucepan over a low heat, stir in the flour and cook gently for 1 minute. Gradually add in the milk, stirring continuously, until thick and smooth. Bring to the boil, stirring, then remove from the heat. Stir in the grated hard cheese and the mustard powder and Worcester sauce, if using. Taste and season. Transfer to a large bowl and leave to cool for 10 minutes.

4. Meanwhile, whisk the egg whites in a clean bowl to stiff peaks.

5. Beat the egg yolks into the cheese sauce. Using a metal spoon, 'stir' in about a third of the whisked egg white to loosen the sauce a little, then fold in the remaining egg whites gently, keeping the air in.

6. Pour the mixture into the prepared souffle dish(es), to come roughly three quarters of the way up the sides. Wipe around the top edge(s) of the dish with your finger, to allow the 'top hat' to form. Transfer the dish(es) to the heated baking tray and bake for 15–18 minutes for the large soufflé or 10–12 minutes for the smaller ramekins. Serve immediately.

Egg Candles

I can't resist using real eggshells as part of my Easter table. I love the natural, earthy style they bring. I've tried all sorts over the years – little quail eggs with flying butterflies in personalised terrariums, soft chocolate ganache in bunny egg cups. This idea is one of my favourites: earthy egg cup candles with added foraged moss. Is there anything that says Easter more?

How to

1. Put the wax pieces in a bowl or pan.

2. Use the microwave or hob to melt the wax. Using the microwave, heat for 20 second intervals at 800w until just liquid. If using the hob, put over a medium heat, keeping a constant eye on it, it should take about 2 minutes. If using essential oils (see Top Tips on the next page), stir them in now.

You will need

- Wax, for melting (Take a guess by eye how much you'll need and any extra can be reserved)
- Bowl or pan
- Microwave or hob
- Essential oils, e.g. lavender, eucalyptus or rosemary (optional)
- Eggs (try different colours and sizes)
- Egg box or egg cups
- Candle wicks
- Cocktail sticks
- Scissors

3. Crack the eggs (carefully) towards the top of the egg and tip the contents into a bowl (no one likes waste!). Carefully break the shell away from the top of the egg, leaving a bowl of shell beneath.

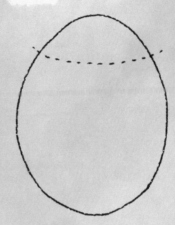

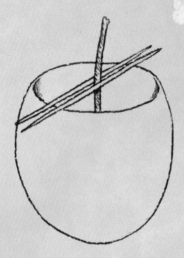

4. Wash and dry the egg shell bowls and stand them in the egg box or int the egg cups.

5. Pour the melted wax into the empty shells.

6. Add a wick to each egg shell and use the cocktail sticks to support the wick in the centre of the candle.

7. Once set, trim the wick to about 1cm (⅓ inch) above the level of the wax.

Top Tips

* Don't overheat the wax; warm it gently until just melting.

* If you fancy using essential oils, make sure the wax is not too hot when you add them, otherwise they evaporate and lose their nice smell.

* Decorate the egg candles in their egg box with moss, or arrange them on a cake stand – have fun with it!

* The egg that you have poured out of the shells can be used to make lunch afterwards . . . have a delicious omelette!

Aromatic Shoulder of Lamb

SERVES
6–8

Spring lamb at Easter is a well-known pairing. This works with mutton, though, too, so just get the biggest shoulder you can.

Ingredients

1 large shoulder of lamb, deboned (roughly 2kg)

2 tbsp extra-virgin olive oil

2 fennel bulbs, trimmed and sliced

12 rainbow carrots, peeled but left whole

3 red onions, quartered

4 garlic cloves, peeled but left whole

a handful of rosemary stalks, bashed

200ml (7fl oz) dry white wine

Methodology

1. Preheat the oven to 170°C/Fan 150°C/338°F. Line a large roasting tin with baking paper.

2. Rub the lamb all over with the olive oil and season with a good amount of salt and pepper.

3. Arrange the fennel slices, carrots, onion quarters, garlic cloves and rosemary stalks in the base of the prepared roasting tin. Place the lamb on top and pour the wine around the sides. Cover the whole tin with foil and transfer to the oven. Cook for 2–3 hours (depending on the size of the shoulder) or until the lamb is meltingly tender. Remove the tin from the oven, leaving the foil in the place, and set aside to rest for 15 minutes.

4. Drain off the pan juices and use a gravy separator to remove the excess fat.

5. Serve the lamb and roasted vegetables with the delicious juices alongside.

Wild Garlic Mash

SERVES
6–8

To think of wild garlic as the weed that keeps giving is so not fair, as it is actually a wild flower. However, it definitely does keep giving. When the leaves arrive, they are beds of wonderful green and the scent is unmistakable, the white flowers are delicate and pretty, and to top it all off every element is edible and tasty.

Ingredients

200g (7oz) butter, diced

50g (1¾oz) wild garlic leaves, finely sliced

1kg (2lb 4oz) high-starch potatoes, such as Russet or Yukon Gold, peeled and cut into equal-sized chunks

50ml (2fl oz) single cream

Methodology

1. Melt 50g of the butter in a sauté pan over a low heat. Add the garlic leaves and wilt gently for a few moments until softened and glossy. Remove the pan from the heat.

2. Meanwhile, place the potatoes in a saucepan of lightly salted cold water. Bring to the boil and cook for 15 minutes, or until cooked through. Drain well, then return the potatoes to the pan. Heat very gently for a moment to dry them out.

3. Pass the cooked potatoes through a potato ricer, then return them to the warm saucepan. Add the remaining butter and the cream to the pan, season with salt and pepper and mash until smooth. Finally, add the wilted garlic and the pan juices to the potatoes and fold gently until combined.

Spring Teacups

Buying vintage teacups is one of my first memories of a car boot sale. I was probably around six or seven years old when I bought my first teacup and now I have thousands. We use them day to day, but also for events – and then there are those with cracks and chips that I keep in my teacup cemetery. There is beauty in imperfection. Add some lovely spring flowers and those lovely teacups have a new life.

You will need

- Teacups
- Soil
- Small plants or spring bulbs
- Moss

How to

1. Use the teacup as a little plant pot.

2. Fill to the top with soil, then add a plant or bulb.

3. Cover the surface with moss to finish.

Top Tips

- Bluebells, small primroses, primulas and daffodils will all work well.

- If you don't have any plants, just add plenty of water to the soil and use flower heads.

- You could use small boxes or jars instead of a teacup.

Decoupage Eggs

These cardboard eggs are so versatile and a really easy way of adding your own personality and style to an Easter table setting. We had an egg decorating breakfast a few years ago, which was great fun. I won't tell you all the details of what happened . . . but hidden somewhere I still have the pictures of how Arthur and Dorothy decorated Dick's head!

You will need

- Flat paintbrush
- Eggs (cardboard ones that open)
- PVA glue
- Feathers

How to

1. Use the flat paintbrush to cover the eggs in PVA glue.

2. Gently position a feather on the egg and cover with PVA glue.

3. Allow to dry.

4. Fill your eggs with Easter goodies.

Top Tips

You can use real eggs that have been blown instead of cardboard if you like.

DYMO NAME TAPES

Add names to make table setting place markers.

How to

1. Use the Dymo printer to print the guest names.

2. Position and stick them on the eggs and trim each egg with coloured string or ribbon tied in a bow.

You will need

- Dymo tape printer and tape
- Eggs (blown or artificial)
- Coloured string or ribbon

Strawberries and Meringues

There are so many ways to make this marriage in heaven look good. We make French meringue, as it is often considered the simplest to make.

Ingredients

4 egg whites

¾ tsp lemon juice

200g (7oz) caster sugar

300g (10½oz) strawberries, destalked and quartered

2 tbsp orange juice

3 tbsp strawberry jam, passed through a sieve

250ml (9fl oz) cream, whipped to stiff peaks

icing sugar, to dust

Methodology

1. Preheat the oven to 110°C/Fan 90°C/225°F. Line a large baking tray with baking paper. Using an 8cm (3¼ inch) cookie cutter as a template, draw 6 circles on the baking paper, then invert the paper (so you can still see the circles) and set aside.

2. Place the egg whites and lemon juice in a large bowl or the bowl of an electric food mixer – make sure it is clean and absolutely grease-free. Whisk the whites until they have doubled in volume and hold a peak. With the whisk still running, add the caster sugar a tablespoon at a time, making sure it is fully incorporated before adding the next spoonful. By the time all the sugar has been added, the whites should be thick and glossy.

3. Spoon the meringue into a large piping bag fitted with a plain nozzle. Pipe concentric rounds inside your drawn circles on the baking paper to form 6 flat base layers. Finally, pipe a ring on top of each outer circle to form a nest shape. Transfer to the oven and bake for about 1½ hours, until crisp and the meringues lift off the paper easily. Leave to cool.

4. About 30 minutes before serving, place the strawberries and orange juice in a bowl.

5. To assemble, spread the base of the meringues with a little strawberry jam. Top with some strawberries, then some whipped cream and finally a few more strawberries. Drizzle over the remaining strawberry jam and serve dusted with icing sugar.

Dorothy's Crème Brûlée

SERVES 6

It doesn't matter how exotic a dessert menu is, we can guarantee that Dorothy will chose the crème brûlée. Even though crème brûlée is French for 'burnt cream', France, England and Spain have all claimed to be the country of its origin.

Ingredients

500ml (18fl oz) double cream

1 vanilla pod, split, or 1 tsp vanilla extract

100g (3½oz) white chocolate, broken into pieces (optional)

6 egg yolks

50g (1¾oz) caster sugar, plus extra for the crunch

Methodology

1. Preheat the oven to 140°C/Fan 120°C/275°F. You will need 6 × 150ml (5fl oz) ramekin dishes.

2. Place the cream and vanilla pod, if using a vanilla pod, in a saucepan. Add the chocolate, if using, and heat gently until it starts to simmer (or until the chocolate has melted).

3. Remove the pan from the heat and scrape the seeds from the vanilla pod back into the cream, or add the vanilla extract, if using. Leave to infuse for 10 minutes.

4. Meanwhile, beat the egg yolks and sugar together in a bowl until pale. Stir in the warm cream, then strain this mixture into a jug. Pour into the ramekins, then place them in a deep roasting tray. Pour boiling water from a kettle to come halfway up the sides of the ramekins, then transfer the tray carefully to the oven and bake for 20 minutes, or until the cream is just set with a still-wobbly centre.

5. Remove the ramekins from the tray and leave to cool, then chill in the fridge for at least 4 hours.

6. To serve, sprinkle some sugar on top of each pudding and caramelise with a blowtorch. The caramel should harden in seconds.

Wild Flower Seed Paper

This craft was inspired by Nathan and Michael's wedding in 2018. They gifted each of their guests a little brown envelope with a handful of their favourite seeds. The message read, 'These flowers will be a memory of our love'. It really touched me, but I love experimenting and thought there must be a way of combining the paper and the seeds . . . Et voila! It's messy and fun and really satisfying! Once the paper is finished, it's quite nice to decorate it with someone's name using simple alphabet stamps. I've often attached a pressed wild flower, too, using some spray glue.

How to make a frame

1. Cut 4 pieces of wood exactly the same length (mine were 20cm/8 inches long).

2. Screw the wood together to make a square.

3. Staple mesh onto one side.

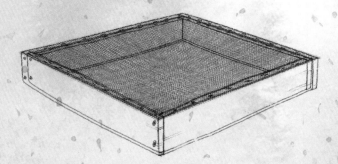

59

Instructions

1. Tear up the scrap paper into small pieces. Place them in the bowl and add some water (enough to cover the pieces). Leave to soak for about 1 hour.

2. Using a blender, liquidiser or hand blender, blitz the paper to make a pulp, adding more water if it gets too thick and draining off some water if it is too runny (see Top Tips below for more info on what the consistency should be). Set aside for another hour.

3. Add the wild flower seeds and mix into the pulp. Pour some of the rested pulp mixture into your tray, just deep enough to allow the frame to be dipped into it.

4. Carefully dip the paper-making frame into the pulp, flattening the frame horizontally under the surface. You will notice the pulp gathering on top of the net. Let it settle as evenly as possible.

5. Remove the frame from the pulp, keeping it flat and horizontal, and allow the water to drain out. Use your fingertips to prize the 4 sides of the pulp away from the edges of the frame for ease of removal and let it drain for a few minutes.

6. Cover a work surface in the tea towels (I usually place down 4 tea towels folded into quarters for extra absorbance) and place the frame on top. The water needs to soak out of the pulp.

7. Use the sponge to push the pulp down onto the frame, soaking up as much of the water as you can from the top surface.

8. Place a dry tea towel alongside, then turn the frame over onto the dry tea towel. Rub the mesh gently with the sponge to release the paper from the frame and onto the towel. Leave to dry overnight.

Top Tips

- The pulp needs to be the right consistency: too runny and it'll need more than one dip and will make thin paper; too thick and the paper will be lumpy.

- You don't need to use a frame, but it's awkward without one and the paper will be uneven.

- Keep the paper flat while it dries.

- You may need to leave the paper overnight to dry thoroughly, but you can speed up the process by placing it in a warm spot.

Rhubarb and Custard Martini

SERVES 6

There is something very elegant about a cocktail served in a martini glass. We love a traditional martini, but this cocktail adds a new dimension with the sweetness of the custard. It is a little too easy to drink so be careful.

Ingredients

450ml (16fl oz) full-fat milk

2 egg yolks

60g (2¼oz) caster sugar

1 tbsp cornflour

1 tsp vanilla extract

ice cubes

6 shots rhubarb liqueur
(or rhubarb gin)

Methodology

1. Heat the milk in a saucepan until it just reaches boiling point. Add in the vanilla extract and remove from the heat.

2. Beat the egg yolks, sugar and cornflour together in a bowl until smooth and pale, then stir in the hot milk. Return the mixture to the saucepan and place over a low heat. Stir for 5–6 minutes until the mixture thickens to coat the back of a wooden spoon. Do not allow the mixture to boil or it will spoil. Remove from the heat and cover the surface of the custard with a piece of clingfilm. Leave to cool and then chill.

3. To serve, place some ice cubes and the rhubarb liqueur into a shaker and shake well until cold. Divide the cold custard between chilled glasses, then pour in the iced liqueur, very carefully over the back of a teaspoon, so it sits on the top of the custard. Enjoy!

Château Shirley Temple

The drink was named after the iconic child actress Shirley Temple. We've included instructions for both an alcoholic and non-alcoholic version here.

Ingredients

2 shots of vodka (for adults)

1 shot of grenadine (for adults)

ice cubes

ginger ale (or lemonade for children)

1 maraschino cherry, to decorate

Methodology

1. If making an adult version, put the vodka and grenadine in a cocktail shaker with ice and shake to chill.

2. Pour into a glass and top up with ginger ale.

3. Add a maraschino cherry to decorate and drink!

 Caution Don't mix up the children and adult versions.

Cherry Blossom Fizz

Inspired to celebrate the Cherry Blossom at the Château, this fragrant cocktail takes you on a visual journey as well as a taste journey!

Ingredients

a dash of cherry liqueur

a dash of Calvados or brandy

a dash of sparkling wine

cherry blossom sprig

Methodology

1. Add a dash of the cherry liqueur and a dash of Calvados or brandy to a champagne glass.

2. Top with chilled sparkling wine.

3. Decorate with as much cherry blossom as is your want. Cheers!

May Celebration

'French' Polpette di Pane

MAKES
24-28
BALLS

(DEPENDING ON SIZE)

There are numerous recipes for using up old bread and, as baguettes are only good for a day (though if you wet them and put them in a 180°C/Fan 160°C/350°F oven for five minutes you can refresh them), we looked around for a way to make a tasty dish other than Pain Perdu. This is great with an aperitif or as the carb element of a light meal.

Ingredients

250g (9oz) stale bread, torn into bite-sized pieces

3 tbsp chopped fresh parsley (or other soft herbs)

1 garlic clove, crushed

200g (7oz) hard cheese, grated (such as Comté)

2 eggs, beaten

vegetable oil, for frying

Make enough!

Methodology

1. Place the bread in a large bowl. Pour in enough warm water to just cover and leave to soak for 5 minutes. Drain the bread in a sieve and squeeze out as much liquid as possible.

2. Place all the other ingredients in a large bowl, season with salt and pepper, and mix well. Add the soaked bread and mix together with a fork until combined. Form into rough balls about the size of a walnut (spiky bits become crunchy bits!).

3. Heat some oil in a deep-fat fryer or an old, high-sided saucepan until it reaches 170°C/338°F on a sugar thermometer. Fry the polpette in batches for 2–3 minutes until crisp and golden.

4. Drain on kitchen paper before serving.

Flatbreads with Grilled Veggies and Hummus

SERVES 6

A lovely light meal or accompaniment to aperitifs – this chapati-style flatbread means flat or slap in Hindi.

Ingredients

FOR THE CHAPATI

225g (8oz) wholemeal flour

½ tsp salt

1 tbsp oil or ghee

FOR THE GRILLED VEGETABLES

2 red, orange or yellow peppers, deseeded and thickly sliced

2 courgettes, trimmed and cut into 5mm/¼ inch slices

1 aubergine, trimmed and cut into 5mm/¼ inch slices

1 red onion, trimmed and cut into 8 wedges

6 tbsp extra-virgin olive oil

1 tbsp herb de Provence mix

a few toasted mixed seeds, to garnish

Methodology

1. To make the chapati, pop the flour and salt into a bowl, then gradually work in the oil or ghee and 125ml (4fl oz) cold water to form a soft dough. Knead for 2–3 minutes (throw down or knead with your fist) until smooth. Cover and leave to rest for 30 minutes.

2. Place the peppers, courgettes and aubergine in a large bowl with the onion wedges and add 2 tablespoons of the oil. Season with salt and pepper and toss together.

3. Place a ridged grill pan over a high heat until hot, add the vegetables in batches and grill for 3–4 minutes, depending on each type, until charred and softened. Once all the vegetables are cooked, pop them back into the bowl. Take a pair of kitchen scissors and cut them up into chunky pieces. Add the remaining olive oil, the herb de Provence and a little more salt and pepper. Stir well and keep warm.

FOR THE HUMMUS

1 × 375g (13oz) can of flageolet beans or chickpeas, drained and rinsed

2 tbsp tahini paste

1 tbsp lemon juice

3–4 tbsp extra-virgin olive oil

4. Meanwhile, make the hummus. Put the beans or chickpeas, tahini and lemon juice in a food processor and blend until smooth. Pour in 3 tablespoons of olive oil and blend again until creamy. Add another tablespoon of olive oil to loosen, if necessary. Season to taste with salt and pepper, cover and set aside.

5. Divide the chapati dough into 6 pieces and shape each one into a round. Place one at a time on a lightly floured surface and roll out to a thin circle approximately 22cm (8½ inches) across. Repeat with the remaining dough, being careful not to coat them with too much flour.

6. Heat a grill pan until hot and cook the chapati one at a time for 1–2 minutes on each side, until cooked through and browned in places. Keep the chapati warm wrapped in a clean tea towel while you cook the others.

7. To serve, spread each chapati with hummus, top with some grilled vegetables and sprinkle with toasted mixed seeds. Fold and eat.

Ribbon Canopy (Maypole)

I've got so many memories of watching people dance around the Maypole. If you are having a spring party, ribbon is a brilliant way of adding a burst of colour. We used a damaged parasol for our 'pole' and a mix of ribbons.

How to

1. Use the drill and metal drill bit to drill a hole 3cm (1¼ inches) into the end of each parasol strut.

You will need

- Drill and metal drill bit
- Old parasol frame (with the fabric removed) and the stand
- String
- Scissors
- Tape measure
- Ribbon – lots and lots of it, different thicknesses and colours
- Cable ties

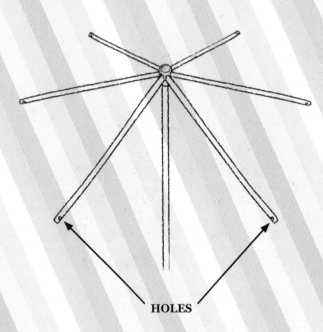

HOLES

4. Measure the length of the struts and the height from the ground.

   Cut some ribbon to twice the length of the struts plus 10cm (4 inches) - 'A'

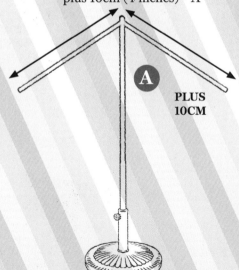

A

PLUS 10CM

2. Open the parasol and place on its stand.

3. Pass a long piece of string through each of the drilled holes. When you come back to go through the first hole, tie both ends of the string securely together.

76

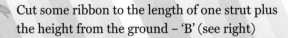 Cut some ribbon to the length of one strut plus the height from the ground – 'B' (see right)

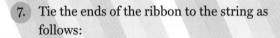 Cut some ribbon to the length of both struts plus the height from the ground – 'C' (see below)

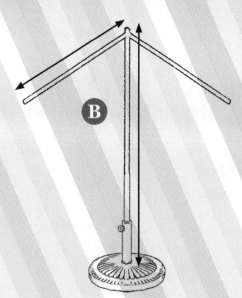

B

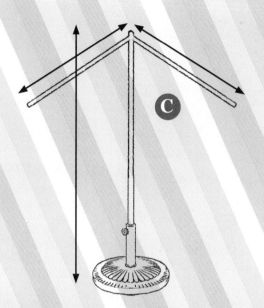

C

5. Bundle the ribbons together in batches of 'A', 'B' and 'C' lengths.

6. Find the centre point of each bundle and secure with a cable tie to the top of the parasol – 'D'.

FASTEN BUNDLE HERE

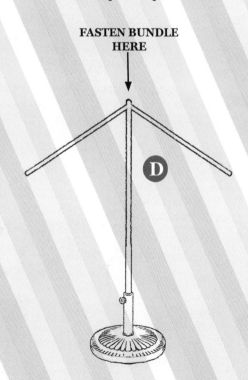

D

7. Tie the ends of the ribbon to the string as follows:

   Ribbon A: Tie both ends of each length of ribbon to opposite sides of the parasol.

   Ribbon B: Tie one end of the ribbon on the string and allow the other end to fall down the centre pole.

   Ribbon C: Tie one end of the ribbon on the string, and the other end on the opposite side of the string and tie where it touches. Then allow the rest of the ribbon to fall to the floor.

   Make sure the hanging ribbons are evenly spaced around the string.

8. Twist the ribbons from 'B' around the centre pole to create a Maypole effect and secure in place.

Wild Flower Hair Garlands

What better way to spend a spring evening than making flower garlands over a cocktail. With a bit of wire and a mix of lovely flowers, you simply cannot go wrong. And once everyone is crowned, it's like fancy dress. Everyone becomes royalty!

How to

1. Measure the thick wire to the circumference of the head. Do not cut the wire to match the circumference of your head, as you will need extra to twist together to secure the garland. Make a kink in the wire, though, to show you roughly what size it will be, and so where you need to embellish.

2. Decorate the straight piece of thick wire with wild flowers. Secure these in place with floral tape, florist glue or thin wire.

3. When you are happy, form the wire into a circle, cut the wire to the correct length and join the ends by twisting them together securely.

4. Use the hairpins to hold the garland securely in place.

Asparagus Tart Tatin

SERVES
4–6

Asparagus only has a short season but they are so delicious and very decadent so we eat them whenever we can.

Ingredients

1 × 230g sheet of ready-rolled puff pastry

400–500g (14oz–1lb 2oz) thin asparagus stems

30g (1oz) butter

100g (3½oz) rashers of smoked streaky bacon, roughly chopped (rind removed, if necessary)

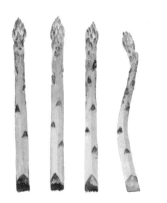

Methodology

1. Preheat the oven to 200°C/Fan 180°C/400°F. Take a 20–22cm (8–9 inch) tatin tin or shallow flameproof casserole dish and trim your puff pastry sheet to be the same diameter. Set aside.

2. Snap the ends from the asparagus stems, then trim the stems so they fit exactly into your prepared tin. Set aside.

3. Place the tatin tin or flameproof casserole dish over a medium-high heat and add the butter and bacon. Fry for 2–3 minutes until golden. Add the asparagus to the pan and cook for 1 minute, turning occasionally and shaking the pan so they cook evenly.

4. Remove the pan from the heat and carefully place the pastry sheet over the asparagus in the pan and press down, tucking the pastry edges under as you go. Pierce the top with a knife to allow the steam to escape and transfer to the oven. Cook for 25 minutes or until the pastry is risen and golden. If the top is becoming too brown, pop a little foil loosely over the top.

5. Remove from the oven and leave to cool for 5 minutes. Finally, upturn onto a plate or board and serve hot.

Pressed Flower Lemon Cake

SERVES
8

The pressed flowers have their own distinct flavours, and combining with a lemon cake allows you to add a citrus dimension to harmonise with the sweetness of the icing. A bought lemon cake seldom delivers the *lemoniness* you want.

Ingredients

FOR THE SPONGE

350g (12oz) unsalted butter, softened

350g (12oz) caster sugar

6 large eggs

grated zest of 4 lemons

500g (1lb 2oz) self-raising flour

1 tsp baking powder

1 tsp salt

50g (1¾oz) soured cream

FOR THE LEMON SYRUP

juice of 4 lemons

10 tbsp caster sugar

Methodology

1. Preheat the oven to 180°C/Fan 160°C/350°F and grease and line two 18cm (7 inch) loose-bottom round cake tins.

2. To make the sponge, place the butter and sugar in a bowl and, using electric beaters, beat together until pale, light and fluffy. Gradually beat in the eggs, one at a time, until evenly combined. Stir in the lemon zest.

3. Sift the flour, baking powder and salt into the bowl, and fold gently until thoroughly mixed. Finally, add the soured cream and fold through.

4. Divide the mixture between the prepared tins and level the surfaces. Transfer to the oven and bake for 40–45 minutes, or until a skewer inserted in the centre comes out clean.

5. Meanwhile, make the lemon syrup. Place the lemon juice and sugar in a small saucepan and heat gently, stirring until the sugar is dissolved. Bring to the boil, then reduce the heat and simmer for 1 minute. Set aside.

6. Remove the cake tins from the oven and place on a wire rack set over a tray. Using a skewer, spike

FOR THE BUTTER ICING

1kg (2lb 4oz) icing sugar, sifted

500g (1lb 2oz) unsalted butter, softened

a few drops of vanilla extract

TO DECORATE

2 sheets of icing flowers

the cakes with holes all over the surface. Very carefully pour the lemon syrup over the cakes, leaving it to soak in. Set aside until the cakes are cooled completely.

7. Meanwhile, to make the butter icing, place the icing sugar and butter in a large bowl with the vanilla extract and, using electric beaters or a food processor, beat together until really soft, light and fluffy.

8. To decorate the cake, remove the cakes from the tins and carefully cut away the rounded tops, using a serrated knife, so that each cake has a flat top. Cut each cake in half horizontally so you have 4 equal layers. Keeping the best of the 2 bases to use as the top, sandwich the cakes together with a thin layer of butter icing. Place the reserved layer on top, then cover the entire cake with the remaining butter icing, spreading it as smoothly and evenly as you can. Using the icing sheet flowers, follow the instructions on how best to apply them to your cake. Transfer to a cake stand and serve!

Flower Cookies

When you make cookies, everyone is your friend. There are so many different recipes, but it is rare to produce a cookie that is also stunning to look at. The dough can be any family recipe, but this one uses one of our favourites which is shortbread based.

Ingredients

100g (3½oz) chilled unsalted butter, diced

75g (2¾oz) icing sugar

200g (7oz) plain flour, plus extra for dusting

a selection of edible flowers

a little caster sugar, to dust

Caution

You can use any edible flowers you like: pansies, rose petals, violas, nasturtium, dianthus and borage blossoms all work well. Parsley or mint leaves would also be good. Remember that the flowers or herbs may add flavour to the cookies, so you want to use varieties that taste as good as they look.

Methodology

1. Place the butter, icing sugar and flour into a food processor and blitz until the mixture resembles fine breadcrumbs.

2. Tip out the mixture onto a lightly floured surface and knead gently until it comes together to form a soft dough. Wrap in clingfilm and chill in the fridge for about 30 minutes.

3. Preheat the oven to 190°C/Fan 170°C/375°F. Line 2 large baking trays with baking paper.

4. Remove the dough from the fridge and roll out on a lightly floured surface to a thickness of about 4mm (¼ inch). Using a round 5cm/2-inch cutter, stamp out cookies and place them on the prepared baking trays. Re-roll the dough, as necessary.

5. Place whole flowers or individual petals on the cookies to decorate and press gently but firmly into the dough. Transfer the trays to the oven and bake for 10–12 minutes, or until the edges have turned slightly golden.

6. Remove from the oven and sprinkle immediately with caster sugar, then transfer to a wire rack to cool.

Rhubarb Syllabub

SERVES 6

It's a fair cop . . . a syllabub is a mix of dairy and alcohol. When the two meet, the acid in the booze, often enhanced with the judicious addition of lemon juice, causes the milk or cream to separate into creamy curds and sweet, tangy whey. Our version has the same taste characteristics but is creamy and smooth.

Ingredients

500g (1lb 2oz) rhubarb, trimmed and cut into cubes

100g (3½oz) caster sugar

125ml (4fl oz) white wine

150g (5½oz) mascarpone

350g (12oz) double cream

75g (2¾oz) icing sugar

Methodology

1. Preheat the oven to 180°C/Fan 160°C/350°F.

2. Place the rhubarb, caster sugar and white wine in an ovenproof dish. Cover with foil and bake in the oven for 20 minutes until the rhubarb has softened. Remove from the oven and set aside to cool.

3. Remove 4 tablespoons of the cooled rhubarb and mash with a fork.

4. Whisk the mascarpone, double cream and icing sugar together in a large bowl to soft peaks, then fold in the mashed rhubarb mixture.

5. Reserving a few of the smaller morsels of rhubarb and a little of the liquor to decorate, divide half the remaining mixture between 6 glasses. Spoon over half the cream mixture, then repeat with a second layer of fruit and cream. Top with the reserved pieces of rhubarb and a drizzle of the cooking liquor. Can be chilled for several hours before serving.

Old-style Lemonade

MAKES
C. 750ML
(1¼ PINTS)

There was lemonade before fizzy pop arrived on the scene!

Ingredients

8 lemongrass stalks, trimmed

225g (8oz) caster sugar

juice of 6 lemons
(approximately 250ml/9fl oz)

Methodology

1. Lightly bash 2 of the lemongrass stalks.

2. Place the sugar in a saucepan and add 250ml (9fl oz) cold water. Heat gently, stirring constantly to dissolve the sugar. Add the bashed lemongrass and bring the mixture to the boil. Simmer for 1 minute, then remove from the heat.

3. Stir in the lemon juice and set aside to cool completely.

4. Discard the bashed lemongrass stalks and pour into a large jug. Add water to taste.

5. Serve in glasses with a lemongrass stalk to stir.

Summer

Summer is a time to pick your harvest, go for picnics and really celebrate the magic of the great outdoors! The sun is shining, the evenings are longer and our minds naturally shift to a more relaxed mode. We go with the flow. The flowers are blooming, the garden is thriving and we are in full event season, too. Having the opportunity to pick flowers direct from the garden for our wedding bouquets is a true gift, and planting perennials like lavender, hydrangeas and dahlias is a lovely way to ensure a ready supply of flowers for your house as well.

Around 21 June the summer solstice occurs; this marks the longest day of the year and the start of summer (even though some argue it is marked by midsummer's day). Summer is the period of maximum temperatures and minimum rainfall and so, while it's a very important season for our events business, we also do our best to enjoy the languid days when the air seems heavy. At the Château in summer, the colours of the land change from bright greens to parched yellows and browns, and we make a conscious decision to follow the Gardens of Heligan technique (a process that encourages plants to send their roots deeper in search of moisture, which enriches the offerings) and refrain from watering our vegetables. It can be a bit nerve racking as you watch your courgettes start to go yellow, but when they find their own water, they come back healthier than ever. We have a monster horseradish plant in the garden, and by summer it is ready to turn into hot horseradish sauce for storing and serving at events. But digging the roots out is never easy as the plants are so robust and the roots are well rooted!

The Château brings us so much joy in the summer, and to keep our family balance we always try to make time to celebrate the simplest of everyday activities, whether that's a garden picnic for lunch or an alfresco dinner in the evening. A summer walk to spot our pollinators is another of our favourite family activities. If you stand still and watch carefully, you will soon see all the bees, butterflies and hawkmoths enjoying nectar in the garden. We once spent nearly two hours watching a carpenter bee doing its work!

By mid-August, the dragonflies and hawkers have invaded the moat and our little pond, along with the swallows that have travelled the best part of 6,000 miles to come and nest in our barns, and we welcome the bats that take the night shift and predate on any flying insects that would like to bite us. We know they are our allies and we love seeing them.

As September rolls around, the brambles are at their juiciest and it's time to start making chutney with our excesses. Not far behind is the sweetcorn. When the golden 'silks' of sweetcorn have turned brown, they should be ready to harvest. Peel back the husks to check that the cobs inside have swollen to their full size and, if you can, cook them within minutes of cutting them to get the sweetest flavours.

Our crafts merge with nature to make every moment feel that bit more special. Jar toppers become the crowning jewel of our harvest, tie-dye table runners and napkins turn a dinner into a party, and summer flower bunting brightens any occasion. We love our summers at the Château and use every spare moment outside enjoying nature and making memories.

Contents

Summer Picnic

Recipes

Crafts

Summer Feasting

Recipes

Crafts

Bounteous Summer squashes

There is something very special about the bounteous squashes that you can harvest in both summer and autumn. With fruits in a wide range of colours, shapes, sizes and flavours, squashes are eye-catching and attractive plants – and from one seed it is possible to get the most amazing amount of produce. Most gardeners make the decision to plant an extra courgette or pumpkin because they have a bit of space left, only to have the 'problem' of where to put all the extra squashes they grow from it. We decided the best way to overcome this problem was to plant a variety of summer and winter squashes. You don't have any less to use or give away, but because they all look a bit different it is somehow easier.

There are lots of ways of describing Cucurbits, but we work on the definition that summer squashes can be eaten, rind, seeds and all. It works for us and we grow: courgettes (round, yellow, green and variegated); cousa squash; patty pan squash (yellow and green); and yellow crookneck squash. These tender plants are easy to grow from seed, are usually sown indoors in spring for transplanting outdoors in early summer, but they can also be sown directly outdoors in early summer. You can grow courgettes in large containers or growing bags in a warm, sunny spot. This is ideal if you have limited space. Water the plant well on planting and continue to water it regularly. If you are growing them in a bed, I would suggest planting in the equivalent of a crater with a thick layer of mulch over the soil around the plant to help hold moisture in the ground. This also speeds up watering

as you have a bowl-like crater to fill. Always harvest your summer squashes when they are small, tender and full of flavour. Regular picking while the fruits are small will ensure a long cropping period.

When it comes to winter squashes, we grow: acorn, spaghetti, turban, potimarron, pumpkin and Jack-o'-lantern. They are grown in a similar way to summer squashes and thrive in rich soil with lots of sun and regular watering. Again, they are usually started from seed indoors in spring, so do need some attention initially, but once settled outdoors, they only really need regular watering. The big difference between the winter and summer squashes, is that winter squashes are usually grown on the ground, as they need plenty of space. We allow the trailing types to sprawl over the ground and we often plant them in the same bed as sweetcorn as it grows up and the winter squashes grow along.

A few interesting facts:

 Squash originated as wild plants in Central America and Mexico.

 While most people consider them a vegetable, if you ask Arthur, he will explain to you that they are, botanically speaking, a fruit – no wonder pumpkin pie is so delicious!

 Squash flowers are edible – they can be eaten fresh, fried, steamed, baked or stuffed with a filling.

Plums and Mirabelles

A tree of plums is a wonderful thing. When ripe, each one is a delight and the trees offer heavy crops of fruit in mid- to late summer. In the walled garden, we have several Victoria plum trees, some French plum varieties and several Mirabelle. I have to admit, before arriving in France, I had never seen a Mirabelle. For our first Christmas at the Château, our neighbour Jacques gave me a bottle of Mirabelle Eau-de-Vie, so I started to take an interest. You can only imagine my surprise to discover there was a whole hedge of Mirabelles adjacent to the main road. No wonder there is so much Eau-de-Vie in this area . . .

A Mirabelle is identified by its small, oval shape, smooth-textured flesh and red or dark yellow colour, which can become flecked in appearance. They are known for being sweet and full of flavour. Every supermarket here sells several kinds of

Mirabelle jam, as 70 per cent of those grown commercially in France are made into jam, while 20 per cent gets turned into Eau-de-Vie. The Mirabelle is harvested once it reaches maturity between July and mid-September. Traditionally, the trees were shaken to cause the fruit to drop. This process is now mechanised, but the principle remains the same: the ripe fruits are shaken loose and collected in a net under the tree. Our trees are quite small, so we shake them by hand.

It is relatively simple to care for plum and Mirabelle trees. They are best planted during the dormant season, before growth starts in late winter or early spring. They like moist but well-drained soil in full sun.

They need little maintenance but should be pruned in early spring or mid-summer to avoid infection by silver leaf disease. In the autumn, it is good to mulch with something rich like home-made compost or well-rotted animal manure.

We have one of our Victoria plum trees against a wall, where the soil is not very good and tends to be dry. So, we dug in a lot of decent compost before planting it and watered it well for its first growing season. This year we have had the most amazing crops of plums and Mirabelle and have been able to ferment over 100 litres of juices to be made into Château Eau-de-Vie.

Cucumbers

I will always remember the first time I planted a cucumber. It was an experiment in an old polytunnel I had bought when I lived in Cornwall, and it was prolific. I must have had fifty cucumbers from a single plant that season and it just kept getting longer and producing more. The more you harvest a cucumber the more fruit it will produce.

It's worth trying to grow cucumbers, even if you don't have a polytunnel. Your season will be shorter, but it's worth it for your own cucumbers. They can be grown in grow bags (two per bag) but you will need to make sure you water them well and regularly. They do not tolerate the cold, so you won't be able to plant them out until late May. There are numerous varieties: the greenhouse-grown ones tend to be long and smooth skinned, whereas outdoor 'ridge' cucumbers have a tougher, rougher skin, and tend to be shorter and fatter. As greenhouse space is limited here at the Château, we tend to grow a single cucumber plant inside and the rest on trellises outside.

If you encourage the plants to climb, you will be able to see your fruit develop and will also get better yields. In the greenhouse we use string and, once the plant has reached the end of its support, we point it in a different direction and allow it to wander around the greenhouse.

Our cucumbers seldom resemble those bought in a supermarket, but they could if we wanted them to . . . Before we left the UK, Angela bought me a couple of Victorian glass cucumber straighteners (essentially long glass tubes that you hang from your plant and can place over the small cucumber as it grows to keep it straight). I did use them once but thereafter decided I'm in favour of wonky fruit and vegetables.

A few interesting facts:

 Cucumbers originate from Southeast Asia.

 They are made up of mostly water – 95 per cent. (Pretty obvious that one!)

 They are a fruit and contain vitamins A, C and B6.

 The flavour actually comes from the seeds.

 A whole cucumber is just 16 calories.

Chillies

The first Europeans to visit the Americas in the late fifteenth century brought back the seeds from the chilli pepper (Capsicum annuum), which are the fruits of Capsicum pepper plants and (as members of the nightshade family) are related to bell peppers and tomatoes. From there, they rapidly spread around the world, and apparently about a third of the world's population now eat chillies at least once a day. Our family love chilli peppers – they are rich in vitamin C, minerals and antioxidants, and help your body absorb iron. It's fair to say Dorothy doesn't like too much heat, but with over 4,000 varieties, you can find a chilli to suit everyone's taste. The 'hottest' part is where the seeds are located, next to the white membrane. Arthur has always had a fascination with chillies . . . maybe it was witnessing the reaction they caused when people ate them!

I find the biggest problem is deciding what chillies to plant. There are a massive variety of seeds available. If in doubt, be conservative with the amount of heat your crop will generate. I suggest a mix: from padron peppers that make a tasty snack when tossed in very hot olive oil and sprinkled with salt, to scotch bonnets where a little goes a long way but the flavour is amazing.

Chillies are tender plants that need heat and sun and grow well in containers. They generally like similar growing conditions to tomatoes, so for the best crop, grow them on a windowsill or in a greenhouse, polytunnel or sunny conservatory. They should also be happy in a sheltered, sun-baked spot outdoors – ideally, beside a south-facing wall or on a sunny patio – although you may get a smaller crop. It's best to sow them indoors between February and April (they need warmth to germinate and have a long growing season), plant them out in June (if you have the right spot for them) and harvest them July to October (it's best to leave them on the plant to ripen, as they mature and the flavour develops). Water them little and often. Make sure you don't overwater them or let them dry out completely.

Our Perfect Summer Breakfast - Patatas a lo Pobre

SERVES 4

It was over twenty years ago that I first heard a description of 'poor man's potatoes' when listening to a storybook CD that I promptly lost. I cooked it from a hazy memory but it is actually close to some of the traditional recipes. We sometimes use leftover, pre-cooked spuds as the whole recipe then only takes about ten minutes.

Ingredients

750g (1lb 10 oz) new potatoes, peeled and thickly sliced

150ml (5fl oz) extra-virgin olive oil

1 whole bulb of garlic, cloves separated but unpeeled

2 onions, roughly sliced

Methodology

1. Pat the potato slices dry using kitchen paper.

2. Heat the olive oil in a good-sized frying pan over a medium heat. Add the potatoes, stirring as you add them to coat them in the oil. Cook for 10 minutes, stirring occasionally.

3. Add the unpeeled garlic cloves, onions and some salt and pepper and stir. Cook for another 15–20 minutes until soft. Adjust the seasoning to taste.

4. Serve the potatoes with their oil, which is to be savoured as well as the potatoes, and there is nothing quite as nice as sucking the soft garlic from the skins.

Gazpacho Shots with or without Sherry

MAKES
20
SHOTS

A Virgin Mary or a Bloody Mary make a great accompaniment to breakfast, so this is that drink in the form of a traditional gazpacho. Add a stick of celery and serve it with or without the alcohol – Sherry in our house – try it! You can add chilli at the start, if you wish.

Ingredients

600g (1lb 5oz) large tomatoes, roughly chopped

1 red pepper, deseeded and roughly chopped

1 cucumber, peeled and roughly chopped

½ small white onion, roughly chopped

4 tbsp extra-virgin olive oil

1 tbsp Sherry vinegar or red wine vinegar

2 slices of white bread, crusts removed (approx. 50g/1¾oz) and torn into pieces

2 tbsp sweet or dry Sherry

a celery stick and pinch of celery salt per person, to serve (optional)

Methodology

1. Place the tomatoes, pepper, cucumber and onion in a blender or food processor and blend until fairly smooth. Add the olive oil and vinegar and blend again for a full 2 minutes until really smooth.

2. Add the bread to the tomato mixture and leave to sit for 10 minutes. Blend again and season to taste with salt and white pepper.

3. Stir in the Sherry and add some iced water if you want a thinner consistency. Refrigerate for at least 1 hour.

4. Serve with a sprinkling of celery salt and a stick of celery, if desired.

Irish Veggie Roll

SERVES 4

This is part of an Ulster Fry and not for vegetarians! Serve this with whatever else you fancy in your fry up – eggs, bacon, mushrooms, tomatoes and, of course, the Patatas a lo Pobre (page 103).

Ingredients

1 tbsp olive oil, plus extra to fry

50g (1¾oz) leeks or spring onions, trimmed, cleaned and finely chopped

500g (1lb 2oz) beef sausagemeat (not minced beef – you need the added fat!)

50g (1¾oz) dried breadcrumbs (such as crushed rusks)

1 tbsp chopped fresh parsley

1 small egg, beaten

½ tsp ground mace, or ¼ tsp mixed spice

Methodology

1. Heat the oil in a small frying pan over a low heat and gently fry the leeks or spring onions for 5 minutes until soft but not browned. Remove from the heat and leave to cool.

2. Tip the cooled leeks or spring onions into a large bowl and add all the remaining ingredients, plus some salt and white pepper. Using your hands, work the mixture together until combined. Cover and leave to rest in the fridge in the bowl for 20 minutes.

3. Turn the mixture out onto a clean work surface and shape into a 'sausage' about 10cm (4 inches) thick. Place in the middle of a piece of clingfilm and wrap the sausage up firmly. Chill in the fridge for 1 hour.

4. Just before serving, slice the sausage into 25mm (1 inch)-thick slices and place some olive oil in a large frying pan over a medium heat. Add the slices and cook for 2–3 minutes on each side until browned. Serve as part of your fry up.

Summer Picnic

Wheaten Bread

Wheaten bread is great for serving with rillettes and using for open sandwiches, as it has a dry consistency and goes well with moist toppings.

Ingredients

450g (1lb) strong wholemeal flour, plus extra for dusting

2 tbsp wheatgerm or oatmeal (optional)

1 tsp cream of tartar

1 tsp bicarbonate of soda

2 tsp caster sugar

½ tsp salt

325–350ml (11–12fl oz) buttermilk or soured milk

Methodology

1. Preheat the oven to 200°C/Fan 180°C/400°F. Lightly grease a baking tray.

2. Mix all the dry ingredients together in a bowl and make a well in the centre. Add 325ml of the buttermilk or soured milk and bring the mixture together until it is a damp but not-too-wet dough, add more buttermilk if needed.

3. Transfer to a lightly floured surface and knead for 2–3 minutes. Shape into a round loaf about 25cm (10 inches) across.

4. Place the dough on the prepared tray and cut a deep cross into the top with a sharp knife. Transfer to the oven and bake for 35–40 minutes, or until the loaf has risen, is a deep golden colour and sounds hollow when tapped on the base.

5. Leave to cool on a wire rack.

Grandma's Falafels

SERVES
8

Using rehydrated chickpeas is the secret to the texture of Grandma's Falafels.

Ingredients

FOR THE FALAFEL

250g (9oz) dried chickpeas
(that have been soaked in a
bowl of water for 24 hours)

1 onion, roughly chopped

1 tbsp each of chopped fresh
parsley, chopped fresh coriander
and chopped fresh dill

2 garlic cloves, finely chopped

¼ tsp each of ground cumin
and ground coriander

a pinch of cayenne

½ tsp baking powder

FOR THE SALSA

3 tomatoes, finely chopped

1 red onion, finely chopped

3 tbsp chopped fresh coriander

juice of 1 lime

sunflower oil, for frying

pitta breads, to serve (optional)

Methodology

1. Drain the chickpeas, then place them in a food
   processor with all the falafel ingredients and process
   until you have a texture like coarse oatmeal. Transfer
   to a bowl and chill for at least 1 hour, but you can
   leave it until the next day.

2. Meanwhile, to make the salsa, combine all the
   ingredients in a small bowl. Season to taste with salt
   and pepper and set aside until ready to serve.

3. Using slightly wet hands, scoop up about 1
   tablespoonful of the falafel mixture at a time, squeeze
   gently and form into walnut-sized balls.

4. Heat about 5cm (2 inches) of sunflower oil in a
   saucepan until it reaches 170°C/338°F on a sugar
   thermometer. Carefully add about 5 falafel balls at a
   time to the hot oil using a slotted spoon and cook for
   3–4 minutes until they are an even golden brown
   (you can give them a little encouragement halfway
   through by turning them over with the slotted
   spoon). Remove with the slotted spoon and keep
   warm, while you continue to cook the rest of the
   falafel in batches.

5. Serve with the salsa and warm pitta breads.

> You can also cook the falafels in an oven preheated
> to 180°C/Fan 160°C/350°F. Just roll the falafels in a
> little oil, then place them on a baking tray and cook
> in the oven at for about 20 minutes until golden.

Caution

Posh Picnic Pasties

James had a pasty company and lives in Cornwall where they are very proud of their pasties, which cannot be called Cornish pasties unless they are made in Cornwall.

Ingredients

750g (1lb 10oz) shortcrust pastry

flour, for dusting

melted butter, to glaze

FOR THE SAVOURY FILLING

150g (5½oz) smoked haddock, skinned and diced

50g (1¾oz) smoked cheese, grated

½ leek, trimmed, cleaned and finely sliced

25g (1oz) butter, finely diced

¼ tsp white pepper

FOR THE SWEET FILLING

200g (7oz) Brie, cut into little pieces (including the rind!)

80g (3oz) your favourite red jam

a little golden caster sugar, for dusting

 Caution

It's all about the crimp!!

Methodology

1. Preheat the oven to 180°C/Fan 160°C/350°F and line 2 baking trays with baking paper.

2. Divide the pastry into 16 equal pieces. Roll out each piece on a lightly floured surface, then cut each one into a round using a 15cm/6-inch plate as a guide.

3. For the savoury filling, mix the smoked haddock, smoked cheese, leek, butter and white pepper in a bowl. Put a small handful of the mixture onto one side of a pastry round, then fold the pastry over the filling. Join the edges together to form a half circle shape. Seal them completely by crimping together. Repeat to make 8 savoury pasties. Transfer the pasties to one of the prepared baking trays and brush generously with melted butter. Set aside.

4. For the sweet filling, divide the Brie between the remaining pastry circles, then top each pile with a dollop of jam. Fold the pastry over the filling, joining the edges together to form a half circle shape. Seal them completely by crimping together. Repeat to make 8 sweet pasties. Transfer the pasties to the second prepared baking tray and brush generously with melted butter. Dust with a little sugar.

5. Transfer both trays to the oven and cook for 30 minutes until golden brown.

Pork, Duck and Salmon Rilettes

The essence of rillettes is meat that has been slow cooked, usually in its own fat, with very little spices or herbs added. When it is cool it should be falling apart. It is then pounded until relatively smooth. Rillettes go well with sourdough bread, crostini, baguettes and Melba toast. And you must serve it with cornichons!

Ingredients

FOR THE PORK RILLETTE

800g (1lb 12oz) pork belly

200g (7oz) pork back fat

2 garlic cloves

2 mace blades

2 bay leaves

FOR THE DUCK RILLETTE

4 duck legs (approx. 350g/ 12oz each)

120g (4¼oz) duck fat

2 bay leaves

6 peppercorns

Methodology

1. Preheat the oven to 150°C/Fan 130°C/300°F.

2. For the pork rillette, place the pork belly skin side up in a roasting tin to fit snuggly. Rub liberally with salt. Gently lift up the pork and arrange the remaining ingredients underneath. Cover the pork with foil and slow roast in the oven for 3 hours, until the meat is meltingly tender. Remove from the oven and leave to cool in the tin.

3. When cool, separate out the meat, discarding the garlic, mace and bay leaves. Chop the meat into 1cm (½ inch) cubes and, using either a large mortar and pestle or a bowl and a rolling pin, pound the meat, adding sufficient fat from the tin to make a rich, velvety mixture. When you are happy with the texture, transfer the rillette to 4 sterilised jars and spread a little of the remaining fat over the top. Seal the jars.

4. Meanwhile, for the duck rillette, keeping the oven to 150°C/Fan 130°C/300°F place the duck legs

FOR THE SALMON RILLETTE

60g (2¼ oz) butter

½ leek, trimmed, cleaned and finely sliced

1 celery stick, trimmed and finely sliced

1 bay leaf

500g (1lb 2oz) salmon with the skin on (tail is good)

2 tbsp lemon juice

½ shallot, finely chopped

1 tbsp finely chopped chives

100g (3½ oz) mayonnaise

skin side up in a roasting tin to fit snuggly with the other ingredients underneath. Rub the legs liberally with salt. Cover the duck with foil and slow roast in the oven for 2 hours, until the meat is meltingly tender. Remove from the oven and leave to cool in the tin.

5. When cool, separate out the meat, discarding the skin and bay leaves. Chop the flesh into 1cm (½ inch) cubes and, using either a large mortar and pestle or a bowl and a rolling pin, pound the meat, adding sufficient fat from the tin to make a rich, velvety mixture. When you are happy with the texture, transfer the rillette to 4 sterilised jars and spread a little fat over the top. Seal the jars.

6. Finally, for the salmon rillette, take a sauté pan that is a little larger than the salmon and add 10g (¼oz) of the butter. Add the leek and celery and fry gently over a medium heat for 3 minutes until soft but not brown. Add the bay leaf, then the salmon, skin side down, and just enough cold water to cover the fish. Add half the lemon juice and bring the water to a simmer. Turn off the heat, cover the pan and leave the salmon to cool completely in the pan juices.

7. Meanwhile, melt the remaining butter in a clean sauté pan. Add the shallot and soften gently over a low heat for 3 minutes. Remove from the heat and stir in the chives, the remaining lemon juice and some salt and white pepper.

8. Flake the salmon flesh into the chive butter, breaking it up gently as you go. Discard the skin and bay leaf. Carefully stir in the mayonnaise, then transfer to 4 sterilised jars. Smooth the surface and seal the jars.

Tea Towels Picnic Bag

There is a romance about a picnic that makes you stop and appreciate your surroundings. We adore them and during lockdown we would have one every week. I always wrap everything in tea towels – they are so useful to protect what you're carrying and also double up as a plate, a serviette and something in which to wrap leftovers. 'What a great idea,' Dick said, 'but wouldn't it be better if it also had handles?'

You will need

- 2 varieties/colours of fabric (I use old tea towels which I cut to size)
- Sewing machine
- Cotton
- Scissors
- Tape measure
- A piece of tape or ribbon 1 metre long

How to

1. Cut 2 × 50cm (20 inch) squares of fabric, one in each type of fabric.

2. Using a sewing machine, with the wrong sides of the fabric together and a 0.5 cm seam, sew the two squares of fabric together all the way around.

3. Cut the tape or ribbon into three pieces – 1 × 68cm (27½ inch) and 2 × 16cm (6¼ inch).

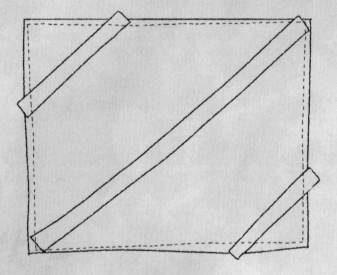

4. To make the bag, start on one side of your square piece of fabric 9cm (3½ inch) from a corner and turn over a 1cm (½ inch) seam.

5. Start sewing along to the first corner. When you get to the first corner, slide one end of the 68cm piece of ribbon or tape under the hem and sew through all layers (this will be your centre strap).

6. Fold over a 1cm (½ inch) seam on the next side of the square and after sewing 41cm (16½ inch) put one end of one of the 16cm (6¼ inch) pieces of tape into the hem and sew through all layers. Finish sewing to the second corner.

7. Fold over a 1cm (½ inch) seam on the third side of the square and after sewing 9cm (3½ inch), put the opposite end of the 16cm (6¼ inch) piece of tape into the hem and sew through all layers. Continue sewing to the next corner once you get to it, Slide the free end of the 68 cms piece of ribbon/tape under the hem and sew into place. This will have created a handle.

Top Tips

Take care in the corners – the layers of fabric will be bulky.

8. Fold over a 1cm (½ inch) seam on the final side of the square and after sewing 41cm (16½ inch), put the final 16cm (6¼ inch) piece of ribbon/tape into the hem and sew through all layers. Continue sewing to the corner. Sew along this first side of the square until you come to just before the 9cm (3½ inch) point where you started, slide the other end of the second 16cm (6¼ inch) piece into the hem and sew through all layers.

Cherry Far Breton

Can be served hot or cold. The traditional Breton dish would use rehydrated prunes.

Ingredients

300g (10½oz) black cherries, pitted

4 eggs

125g (4½oz) caster sugar

125g (4½oz) plain flour

a pinch of salt

50g (1¾oz) unsalted butter, melted

50ml (2fl oz) cold milk

25ml (1fl oz) dark rum

Methodology

1. Preheat the oven to 200°C/Fan 180°C/400°F. Lightly butter a 1 litre (1¾ pint) baking dish.

2. Arrange the cherries in the bottom of the prepared dish.

3. Place the eggs and sugar in a bowl and whisk with a balloon whisk until pale and creamy. Sift in the flour and salt, and stir well until the batter is smooth. Add the melted butter, milk and rum and beat again until smooth and slightly glossy.

4. Pour the batter over the cherries in the dish and transfer to the oven. Bake for 10 minutes, then reduce the heat to 170°C/Fan 150°C/338°F, and continue to cook for a further 20 minutes, until the batter is firm and the top golden. Remove from the oven and leave to cool to room temperature.

5. Serve with cream, if wished.

DIY Sunshade and Dressing

This very simple shade can roll up to fit snugly under your arm or will fit into the crowded boot of your car. I used an old pair of curtains to make ours. You can even spray it with a waterproof sealant, so that you don't get a soggy bottom when the heavens open!

How to

1. Cut the bamboo or wooden broomstick/pole to the following lengths:

   ❖ 1 × the same length as the width of your fabric

   ❖ 2 × the height you want the shade

2. Sew a nice, neat hem around the edges of the fabric.

3. Fold the fabric in half along the long side to mark the centre point of your tent. Draw a line across the centre of the fabric.

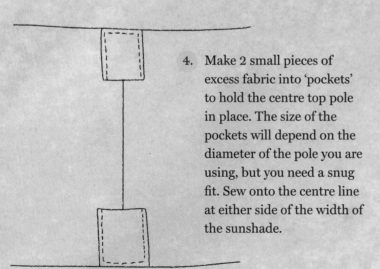

4. Make 2 small pieces of excess fabric into 'pockets' to hold the centre top pole in place. The size of the pockets will depend on the diameter of the pole you are using, but you need a snug fit. Sew onto the centre line at either side of the width of the sunshade.

You will need

- Bamboo or wooden broomstick/pole (the size depends on how big you want your finished shade to be)
- Saw
- Tape Measure
- Pencil
- Fabric panel (mine was 130 × 250cm/51 × 98 inches)
- Sewing machine
- Cotton
- 4 eyelets
- 4 pieces of cord
- Drill and drill bit (this should be the same diameter as the dowel)
- Wood adhesive/ strong adhesive
- 2 small pieces of dowel
- Hammer
- 4 tent pegs
- An old pair of curtains

5. Attach an eyelet to each corner of the fabric.

6. Attach a piece of cord to each eyelet (these will be the guide ropes).

7. Place the longest pole into the pockets. Make a small mark on each end of the pole, just beyond the pockets.

8. Remove the pole and, using the drill and drill bit, drill small holes in the centre pole at the marked points.

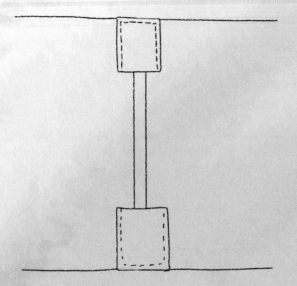

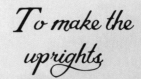

To make the uprights

1. Drill a hole in the top of the 2 upright poles.

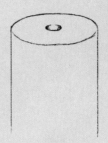

2. Fill the hole with adhesive and push the dowel into the hole.

3. Replace the centre pole in the pockets and insert one upright into each of the holes. Use the tent pegs to secure the cords into the ground to stabilise the shade and hold everything down securely.

Ginger Beer

This is mildly alcoholic as the ginger is fermented but we've never tested to see exactly how alcoholic

Ingredients

TO START

75g (2 ¾oz) ginger root, cut into strips using a potato peeler, then bashed with a mortar and pestle

Zest and juice of ½ a lemon

25g (1oz) sugar

TO FEED

Sugar

Powdered ginger or diced and crushed fresh ginger

TO FINISH

200g sugar (7fl oz)

2 x 1 litre fizzy drink bottles

Mildly alcoholic and should be used within a couple of weeks.

Methodology

1. Place the bruised ginger, lemon zest and juice, and the sugar into a glass jar and cover with warm water (approx. 200ml/7fl oz should suffice).

2. Swirl around to dissolve the sugar.

3. Set the lid loosely on the jar (we use a sauerkraut jar – the lid sits on top with a little water to allow gases to escape when it starts to ferment).

4. Leave in a warm place for 48 hours.

5. Feed daily for a week with a teaspoon of sugar and a teaspoon of ginger and mix well. The ginger beer will bubble due to the natural yeast on the ginger root.

6. After a week, strain the liquid off your ginger root mix. You will use ¾ for your first batch of ginger beer and top up the remaining ¼ to 200ml (7fl oz) and feed it daily as before. (Every week you can use ¾ of this starter for another batch of ginger beer).

7. Dissolve 200g (7oz) of sugar in just under 2 litres (3 ½ pints) of water and allow to cool. Add the strained ¾ of your ginger beer starter and put into 2 x 1 litre fizzy drink bottles. Screw on the top (they have to be fizzy drink bottles to withstand the pressure of the Carbon Dioxide produced by the yeast). After 5 days at room temperature, place in the fridge. This slows fermentation and once chilled they are ready to drink.

Elderberry Fizz

When our elderflowers are in bloom the walled garden is filled with the most amazing floral bouquet.

Ingredients

500g (1lb 2oz) elderberries, picked from stalks

juice of 1 lemon

approximately 600g (1lb 5oz) caster sugar

fizzy water, chilled, to serve

Methodology

1. Wash the elderberries and shake dry. Place in a saucepan and add enough water to just cover them. Bring to the boil, reduce the heat and simmer gently for 15 minutes, or until the berries have softened. Remove from the heat and leave to cool for 10 minutes.

2. Strain the liquid through a fine sieve and discard the berry mush. Measure how much liquid you have and transfer to a clean saucepan. Add the lemon juice and 400g (14oz) of sugar for every 500ml (18fl oz) of liquid. Bring to the boil, then reduce the heat and simmer for 10 minutes. Remove from the heat and allow to cool completely.

3. Transfer to a bottle.

4. To serve, pour plenty of cordial into a large jug and top with some cold fizzy water.

Watermelon and Lime Refresher

Ingredients

wedge of watermelon, cut into thick slices or chunks

4–6 limes, cut into thin wedges

Methodology

1. Place the watermelon and lime wedges into a large jug and add some iced water. Leave to steep in the fridge for 1 hour or so.

Summer Feasting

Oatcakes For Cheese Board

Home-made oatcakes are easy and transform a cheese board, especially in France where they don't even have crackers!

Ingredients

225g (8oz) oatmeal (or ground-up porridge or rolled oats)

60g (2¼oz) wholemeal flour

1 tsp fine salt

½ tsp granulated sugar

½ tsp bicarbonate of soda

60g (2¼oz) butter, chilled and cubed

70–80ml (2½–3fl oz) hot water

Methodology

1. Preheat the oven to 190°C/Fan 170°C/375°F. Line a baking tray with baking paper.

2. Mix the oatmeal, flour, salt, sugar and bicarbonate of soda together in a bowl. Add the butter and rub together with your fingertips until it is the consistency of large breadcrumbs. Stir in the hot water and bring the mixture together to form a soft, slightly sticky dough.

3. Roll out the dough on a lightly floured surface until it is about 4–5mm (¼ inch) thick. Using a 7cm/2¾-inch cookie cutter, stamp out rounds and place them on the prepared tray. Re-roll the dough as necessary until you have approximately 20 oatcakes.

4. Transfer the tray to the oven and bake for 15–20 minutes, or until lightly golden. Allow the oatcakes to cool on the tray for several minutes before transferring to a wire rack to cool completely.

Summer Pickles

These pickles are good for a week.

Ingredients

FOR THE PICKLES

cauliflower, broken into florets

red, orange and/or yellow small sweet peppers, sliced into rings

1 red onion, sliced through the roots

1 fennel bulb, finely sliced

baby sweetcorn, sliced lengthways

rainbow-coloured carrots, finely sliced at an angle or with a peeler

FOR THE PICKLING LIQUEUR

500ml (18fl oz) vinegar

500g (1lb 2oz) caster sugar

1 tsp peppercorns

½ tsp mustard

½ tsp salt

Methodology

1. Mix all the pickle vegetables in a large bowl, then pack them into sterilised jars, so they look interesting.

2. To make the pickling liqueur, combine the vinegar, caster sugar and 500ml (18fl oz) of water in a saucepan. Add the peppercorns, mustard and salt and heat gently. Pour the pickling liqueur over the vegetables and seal the jars.

Chargrilled Avocado and Salsa

SERVES 4–6

Arthur and Dorothy love to remind us that apparently you can survive if your diet is just avocados! We love them and are always looking for ways to include them in our meals. Chargrilling the rich smooth avocados adds a caramelised dimension that is wonderful with the texture and tastes of a fresh, home-made salsa. This is a winner if you have vegan friends coming to your barbeque.

Ingredients

1 avocado per person, halved and stone removed

FOR THE SALSA

3 tomatoes, diced

1 red onion, diced

3 tbsp chopped coriander leaves

juice of 1 lime

1 Scotch bonnet chilli, deseeded and finely diced

Methodology

1. To make the salsa, place all the ingredients together in a bowl, season with salt and freshly ground black pepper, then mix well.

2. Chargrill the avocado until nicely marked and fill with salsa to serve.

Tie Die Fabric

Since moving to France, I've become obsessed with French linen. I buy all sorts, but my favourites are the monogrammed white napkins. We use them all the time but, like anything white, they take an effort to keep clean. Cue the idea for ombre dying: it adds a nice pop of colour and also hides a multitude of sins!

You will need

- Plastic sheet or similar
- Fabric dye
- Big plastic container
- White napkins, a table runner or a tablecloth (cut/torn into strips)
- Coat hanger with clips (ones you would use for trousers)
- Rubber gloves (wear them the whole time!)

How to

1. Ensure your working area is protected from the dye – so cover it with a plastic sheet or similar.

2. Mix the dye in a big plastic container according to the packet instructions.

3. Thoroughly wet your napkins, table runner or torn tablecloth with cold water and wring out.

4. Flatten the fabric out carefully, then fold so that only the part of the cloth that is going to be dyed is at the bottom.
Clip the top of the folded cloth onto the coat hanger, letting the fabric below hang loose.

5. Make sure you are wearing rubber gloves and dip the part of the fabric that you want to colour into the dye bath.

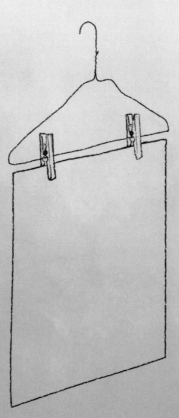

6. Leave the fabric in the dye for a few moments, then lift out and let the dye drain off back into the dye bath.

7. Repeat the dipping and draining process, placing progressively less fabric in the dye bath. What will happen is that the highest part of the dyed fabric, which has only been in the dye bath once, will be lighter than the bottom of the dyed fabric, which has been in the dye bath multiple times.

8. Once you are happy with the colour gradient, lift the fabric away from the dye bath and allow it to drain as much as possible.

9. Squeeze out any excess dye.

10. Remove the fabric from the coat hanger, open it out and rinse with cold water until the water runs clear.

11. Peg the fabric out to dry.

Top Tips

❀ WEAR RUBBER GLOVES, unless you want your hands to be the same colour as your napkins!

❀ Be patient – the whole process may take a good 30 minutes. If you rush, the dye won't be strong and it might be uneven.

❀ Make sure you buy dye that is appropriate for the fabric. Most dyes are for cotton or natural fibres and won't work on polyester/polycotton mixes.

❀ Use a little scrap piece of fabric to practise first, in order to see how the colour holds/takes to the fabric.

❀ To achieve the effect of the table runner (see page 136) fold the table runner corrugated lengthwise, clip onto the coat hanger and then have fun dipping the fabric at different angles.

❀ Be careful before the dye is washed out – if a dyed area touches a non-dyed area, colour will be transferred.

❀ Dye the fabric a little darker than you want the fabric to be, because some of the dye will wash out on rinsing.

❀ Follow the packet instructions and always use a fixative to make sure your tie die lasts.

❀ Be creative – I've used a stained, thick, linen tablecloth before. I cut it to the desired size and even kept the raw edges!

❀ Iron the material well before use.

Jelly Bag Cocktail

MAKES
1 LITRE
(1¾ PINTS)

When you make jelly from your own fruit, you know that you shouldn't squeeze the bag to extract the last bit as it makes your conserve cloudy, however, we always squeeze and bottle the last bit as a 'family only' perk . . . even after you have squeezed the last bit you know there is more, sweet flavour left, hence we came up with the idea of steeping the leftover fruit and sugar in alcohol to make our jelly bag liqueur.

Ingredients

softened blackcurrant from making blackcurrant jelly

1 bottle of vodka

Champagne or fizzy water, to serve

Methodology

1. Spoon the contents of your jelly bag (after bottling the jelly itself) into a sterilised bottle and top up with the vodka, making sure you cover all the mush. Leave to infuse for 1 month (or longer) until you have a rich, blackberry-flavoured vodka liqueur.

2. To serve, pour a little of the liqueur into glasses and top up with Champagne or fizzy water.

Château Caesar Salad

Caesar salad was invented in the early 1920s by Caesar Cardini, an Italian chef who owned a restaurant in Tijuana, Mexico.

Ingredients

125g (4½oz) day-old baguette or sourdough, cut into 2cm (¾ inch) chunks

3 tbsp olive oil

4 small chicken breast fillets

2 Romaine lettuce or 6 Little Gem lettuces, leaves separated

50g (1¾oz) marinated white anchovies in oil, drained

Parmesan shavings, to serve

FOR THE DRESSING

1 garlic clove

2 anchovies in oil, drained

2 tbsp freshly grated Parmesan

5 tbsp mayonnaise

1 tbsp white wine vinegar

Methodology

1. Preheat the oven to 180°C/Fan 160°C/350°F.

2. Place the bread chunks in a bowl. Add 2 tablespoons of the oil and a little salt and pepper. Toss well until they are all lightly coated. Transfer the bread to a baking tray and bake in the oven for 8–10 minutes, until evenly golden and crisp. Set aside to cool completely.

3. Brush the chicken fillets with the remaining oil and season with salt and pepper. Place a ridged grill pan over a high heat until hot, then add the chicken breasts and fry for 3–4 minutes on each side, until cooked through and evenly charred. Transfer to a sheet of foil, wrap loosely and set aside to cool completely.

4. Meanwhile, to make the dressing, place the garlic and anchovies in a mortar with a pinch of salt. Pound gently with a pestle until a paste is formed. Transfer to a small bowl and stir in the Parmesan, mayonnaise and vinegar until evenly combined. If necessary, thin with a drop or two of boiling water – it should have the consistency of thickened pouring cream.

5. To assemble the salad, cut the chicken into thin slices and place in a large bowl with the lettuce and croutons. Top with the anchovies and some Parmesan shavings, and drizzle over the dressing to serve.

Braised Summer Squashes

SERVES 8

A great way to use up any surplus squash you might have.

Ingredients

75g (2¾oz) butter

1kg (2lb 4oz) mixed yellow and green squash, trimmed, deseeded and cut into equal-sized pieces roughly 2cm (¾ inches)

2 garlic cloves, thinly sliced

125ml (4fl oz) hot chicken stock

Methodology

1. Melt 50g (1¾oz) of the butter in a large braising pan over a gentle heat. Add the squash pieces and garlic and sauté gently for 5 minutes without browning (you may need to do this in batches).

2. Add the stock to the pan and simmer gently over a medium heat for 3–5 minutes, until the squash is just tender.

3. Add the remaining butter, season with salt and pepper and shake lightly. Serve at once.

Fish Crudo

SERVES 8

Simple and healthy, it looks lovely and tastes refreshing.

Ingredients

300g (10½oz) firm white fish fillets, such as hake, cod, whiting or haddock

juice and zest of 1 lemon

1 tbsp capers

2 radishes, trimmed and finely sliced

a few micro herbs

extra-virgin olive oil, to drizzle

Methodology

1. Pop the fish into the freezer for about 1 hour prior to serving. (The fish is far easier to cut into wafer-thin slices when it is semi-frozen.)

2. Slice the fish into thin slices, then place them on a serving board. Squeeze the lemon juice all over and top with the lemon zest, capers, sliced radishes and micro herbs. Drizzle liberally with olive oil and season with flaked salt and cracked pepper. It is ready to serve.

Château Mixed Grill

SERVES 8

This is a meat fest with easy-to-share cuts and Adana (spiced lamb skewers) from South Turkey.

Ingredients

600g (1lb 5oz) sirloin or rib eye beef steak, cut into 16 large chunks

8 small banana shallots, peeled but left whole (see tip)

1 large courgette, trimmed and cut into 8 chunks

1 large red pepper, deseeded and cut into 8 chunks

olive oil, for greasing

400g (14oz) minced lamb

2 tsp ras el hanout (or your favourite spice)

1 tbsp chopped fresh mint

4 small poussins

a small handful of fresh herbs, such as rosemary, thyme and sage (optional)

8 padron peppers

8 Toulouse sausages

You will need 8 bamboo skewers

Methodology

1. For the beef kebabs, thread 4 chunks of beef and 2 pieces of each vegetable on 4 large skewer. Rub all over with oil, and season with salt and pepper. Set aside.

2. For the lamb skewers, place the minced lamb in a bowl with the ras el hanout or other spice, fresh mint and a good amount of salt and pepper. Using your hands, mix together well until thoroughly and evenly combined. Divide into 4 and shape each quarter into a long sausage about 15cm/6 inches long and 2cm (¾ inch) in diameter. Thread each one onto a skewer and set aside.

3. For the poussins, truss each one up with string. If you like, you can pop a few fresh herbs into each cavity before trussing. Rub the skins with oil, and season with salt and pepper.

4. For the padron peppers, rub them with olive oil and season with salt and pepper.

5. Lightly prick the sausages.

6. You now have all your meat ready to be chargrilled on your barbecue or in a smoker. The poussin will take the longest time to cook – up to 30 minutes, turning frequently over hot coals – so start with these. Sausages will take around 20 minutes. Both sets of kebabs will take between 12 and 15 minutes, turning a couple of times. The peppers will take the least amount of time and can be added last. They will take 3–4 minutes on each side over hot coals.

7. Always rest the meat for a good 10 minutes before serving.

Bloomin Lovely Summer Flower Bunting

Whether you hang dried flowers, fresh flowers or foliage from the garden, one thing you can be sure of is that summer flower bunting will put a smile on your guests' faces. And, at the end of the party, you can let them take the flowers home as favours (it saves you the job of taking them down!).

How to

1. Decide on the position of your dining table – you will need to think about how/where you will be able to secure the bunting string/cord, especially if you want the bunting to hang over/around the table. You will need there to be trees, a fence or a wall/post to attach the bunting.

2. Tie the bunting string/cord over/around the table – pay attention to the height of the string, as no one wants to bump into the hanging flowers.

3. Use the 'S' hooks to hang the flowers from the bunting string/cord. We simply hung the flowers using the leaf nodes coming off the stem or the flower itself.

You will need

- Long, strong string or cord (a washing line is perfect)
- Metal hooks ('S' type – we use roof tile hooks)
- Lots of flowers (enough to cover the length of your string or cord and give you the display you envision)

Top Tips

- Use any seasonal summer flowers, foliage, or seed pods, etc. We used artichoke heads, gladioli, sweet peas, lupins, eucalyptus fronds and sunflowers.

- Hang the flowers at different heights and mix them up.

- If using fresh flowers, add them last so that they remain as fresh as possible.

- Put your leftover flowers in jars and vases. You can never have enough!

Jam Jar Toppers for Preserves from the Garden

You will need

- Fabric scraps
- Scissors/pinking shears
- Home-made preserves or mini jars of honey
- Rubber bands
- Coloured cord/jute/ribbon
- Labels and a pen (for the table settings)

As a family, we love preserving and, with a little bit of care and crafting magic, you can transform a simple but very tasty jar of garden goodness into a special gift. You can also create lovely table settings with mini jars of honey, some labels and these toppers. You only need a very small piece of fabric, so I keep all scraps. Dorothy's favourite is one she made with a pair of Dick's torn pants. For some reason it's still untouched in our preserve cupboard!

How to

1. Cut circles of fabric to cover the jam jar lids – 3cm (1¼ inches) bigger than the lid's diameter.

2. Place the fabric on top of a jar of home-made preserve or a mini jar of honey and secure it in place with a rubber band.

3. Tie some coloured cord, jute or ribbon around the rubber band to cover it.

4. If you are making the table settings, add labels and write on the guests' names.

Top Tips

When you are making home-made preserves, don't forget to add nice labels so that everyone knows what is in the jars! Be sure to include the date that the preserve was made.

If your fabric scraps are plain, decorate them before securing them to the jar by painting small fruits or veggies using fabric paint or ink stamps.

Plum Tatin

Sweeter than apples and juicier, too.

Ingredients

1 packet of ready-rolled puff pastry

75g (2¾oz) caster sugar

75g (2¾oz) butter, chilled and diced

10–12 plums, halved and stones removed

vanilla ice cream, to serve

Methodology

1. Preheat the oven to 180°C/Fan 160°C/350°F. You will need a tatin dish or a flameproof casserole dish about 23cm (9 inches) in diameter.

2. Unroll the pastry onto a flat surface. Carefully place the tatin dish in the centre. Using a sharp knife, cut the pastry to the same size as the dish. Transfer the pastry to a baking tray, prick it all over with a fork and rest it in the fridge until required.

3. Place the sugar in a small saucepan and add 1 tablespoon of cold water. Place over a gentle heat, stirring until the sugar dissolves. Do not let it boil. As soon as all the sugar is dissolved, stop stirring, increase the heat and simmer the sugar syrup for 2–3 minutes, until it starts to turn a lovely golden brown (remember not to stir once the liquid simmers).

4. Remove the saucepan from the heat and immediately stir in the butter. It will bubble up nicely, but simply stir with a wooden spoon. Once mixed, pour the caramel sauce into the tatin dish. Arrange the halved plums in the caramel, cut side down, placing them around the edge of the dish first to fit very tightly, then fill in the middle in a similar fashion. Gently press with your hands to ensure there are no gaps.

5. Remove the pastry from the fridge and carefully press it down over the plums, tucking the pastry edges under as you go. Transfer to the oven and bake for 30–35 minutes, until the pastry is golden brown and crisp.

6. Allow to cool for 10 minutes before running a knife around the edge of the dish and inverting the tatin onto a large serving plate. Be careful at this stage, as there will be a lot of hot juice. Serve with vanilla ice cream.

Autumn

A utumn comes slowly to our part of France. The leaves can hang on for months. But then, towards the end of October, we suddenly realise there are amazing autumnal colours to enjoy. Not long after, we have leaves to sweep up. By the time we have had the autumn equinox, around 21 September, the days are markedly shorter and it feels a lot cooler.

Summer slides into autumn and we cherish every evening when the nights are still warm enough to sit outside. Warm autumn evenings feel like a gift – we expect them from May to September, but by October they are a treat to be celebrated. There is always the moment when we have to put on that extra layer of clothing, and then we add our overcoat, and then our scarves! Autumn walks, crunching leaves and hot chocolates replace picnics and pollinator spotting. And for Arthur and Dorothy, October is dedicated to Halloween preparations!

During these months we grow lots of pumpkins and squashes to be used through the winter period – as well as ensuring we have plenty for Halloween, obviously. These celebrations have become a real feature of our year at the Château, with the children's

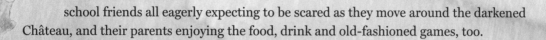

school friends all eagerly expecting to be scared as they move around the darkened Château, and their parents enjoying the food, drink and old-fashioned games, too.

Halloween is not really for us, so Dick and I want to ensure that our children also have wonderful memories of bonfire night. Jacket potatoes, home-made baked beans and warm drinks by the fire are the memories I cherish. The children love the silly games, toasted marshmallows and toffee apples!

We had our wedding in glorious sunshine in the middle of November, the first year we moved into the Château, and our wedding anniversaries have largely been celebrated in good weather since then. Back in the UK, I was always aware of the race to get the first bottles of Beaujolais Nouveau, after it is released on the third Thursday of November. It comes from the Beaujolais region of France and is made using a process called carbonic maceration, which results in a wine that is light-bodied, fruity and easy to drink when it is young. I stopped thinking about it when we moved to France and now take it as a given that every supermarket will magically have stocks instantaneously upon release.

I used to think autumn was the filler between summer celebrations and Christmas, but now I fully understand the joy that this season brings. It is unexpected and magical and has given us some very special family memories.

'No shade, no shine, no butterflies, no bees, No fruits, no flowers, no leaves, no birds— November!'

Thomas Hood (1799–1845), British poet

Contents

Autumn Feasting

Recipes

Crafts

Bonfire Night

Recipes

Crafts

Leeks

Leeks are alliums (members of the onion family). They're not romantic, but they are versatile, very satisfying and easy to grow (although it can take five months from planting to harvesting). A couple of things you may not know about leeks: they are native to the Middle East and the eastern Mediterranean; humans have been consuming them for over 6,000 years; they are rich in antioxidants, potassium and iron; and they are a popular salad vegetable . . . Yes, they can be eaten raw! The stems are, in fact, bundled white leaf sheaths and, though many prefer to just use the white stalk, the whole plant is tasty.

Maybe it's my military background, but there is something I find so satisfying about seeing a row of leeks in the garden. I know they can be grown in messy beds but what would the Sergeant Major say?! Some of my earliest gardening memories are of planting leeks with my dad back in Northern Ireland nearly sixty years ago. He learned how to plant them from his dad, and I have now taught Arthur and Dorothy to plant them in the same way . . . Twist off the green tops before replanting the seedlings. It is a proven method for growing strong and tasty leeks, and I think it is lovely that the tradition carries on long after my grandpa and dad have left us.

The best time to start cultivation is during the second half of spring. You can start your seeds off in pots or seed trays, but the easiest way to get your leek crop going is by planting seeds directly in the ground. It's gardening, so you have to prepare the ground first (something Arthur and I love doing together!). I always sow in a 'drill' and, even though the plants will eventually need to be 15cm (6 inches) apart, make sure you start with many more seeds. When the seedlings resemble thin spring onions and are tough enough to be handled, ease a trowel into the side of the drill and lever up the plants, loosening the roots. Gently pull out the weaker plants. These 'thinnings' can then be replanted to make several more rows, or put into a 'lazy bed' (see next page).

To plant the seedlings, take a bundle of the young plants firmly in one hand and, using the other hand, hold the green tops and twist to remove approximately half the green leaves. You now have shortened seedlings. Next, use your dibber to make holes to the depth of the white on your seedlings approximately 15cm (6 inches) apart. Drop them in, press down the soil around your seedlings and water to set the roots back into the earth. To increase the amount of the more tender white stem on the plant, you can add more soil to cover the exposed white part of the plant as it grows.

To make a 'lazy bed', push your spade in to full depth in your prepared ground, then push forward to reveal a gap behind the blade. Place any un-planted seedlings

vertically side by side in this gap, then ease out the spade and push the soil back against the seedlings. Again, water them to set the roots. You now have a line of leeks that are far too close for conventional wisdom but will provide you with a delicious crop of smaller leeks.

Carrots and parsnips

Parsnips and carrots are part of the same family and both are ubiquitous in the autumn. In our garden, carrots are available all the way through the summer, initially as young tender baby carrots, and then latterly as large mature carrots destined for roasting, broths

and stews. Parsnips, however, grow through the summer and are ready to be eaten in the autumn and all the way to the end of winter, when they have to be pried from the frozen ground to be taken indoors to be cooked. Both vegetables are delicious and versatile, and carrots are now readily available in lots of different colours, from white, yellow and orange, to purple and even variegated varieties.

Carrots are relatively straightforward to grow from seed and, if you like to eat them small, sow them in small batches regularly from early spring onwards. It may come as a surprise to you, but home-grown carrots are not always as straight and uniform as supermarket carrots. This can happen because the soil is too stony, or because the soil is too rich. However, don't worry about that, as they taste so much better. They are also drought-resistant, so will rarely need watering. The main pest you come across with carrots and parsnips is the carrot fly, whose larvae will tunnel into your carrots. We grow ours in rows with garlic, leeks or onions between them, as the carrot fly is kept at bay by the strong scent of the onions or garlic.

Parsnips are low maintenance and a must for any vegetable grower. They are slow growing, and you should wait until the soil has warmed up in May before sowing plenty of seeds directly into their growing position.

Apart from weeding when the plants are young, they take little maintenance. It's best to wait until after the first frost before you harvest as, that way, you'll get the sweetest flavour. Because they are very hardy, parsnips can be left in the ground right through winter.

How to do it:

 Prepare your drill.

 Scatter the seeds thinly along the drill (germination can be unreliable so it's best to sow more than you need).

 Cover the seeds with soil and water.

 Keep well weeded, then thin when the seedlings are well established.

Apples

Having spent our first year at the Château doing mainly essential restoration, electrics, plumbing and sewage works, it was during our first winter that we discovered French supermarkets sell fruit trees in the planting season. We bought ten in the 'end of line' sale for about €8 each, which forced us to address the laying out of the walled garden. We excavated some of the original paths and planted trees so that one day they would line our pathways. Nearly ten years on, our last season produced a prolific quantity and variety of fruit, so much so that we built traditional beech apple storage cupboards in the cellars to store them.

Apples are probably the easiest and most popular fruit tree to grow and there are many varieties, each with their own unique texture and flavour. Some people estimate there are more than 30,000 varieties of apple worldwide, with at least 7,500 cultivated varieties of eating apple. Whether you have inherited a tree or an orchard, or have decided to plant your own, enjoy the time you have together from buds and blossoms, through to bountiful fruiting and dormant winters. There is something very special about harvesting from your own fruit trees and, compared to other crops, they will produce delicious harvests for decades with relatively little work apart from pruning and dealing with any pests. There is nothing quite like eating a crisp, juicy apple straight from your own tree in the autumn, or going to your fruit store in mid-winter and selecting an apple that has matured over the months and is now even sweeter.

If you are planting apple trees for the first time, you need to decide if you want a dessert apple, a cooking apple or a dual-purpose apple. As we had the space, we went for all three types. One very important thing to consider when you are choosing the variety to plant is the flowering time. Unless you buy a self-pollinating variety (it should say so on the label), you will need more than one fruit tree, you will need them to blossom at roughly the same time and you will need to plant them relatively close to each other (within 20m/65ft is good), to help the pollinators do their job.

The best time to plant young apple trees is while the tree is dormant, from late autumn

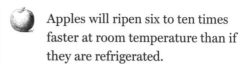
Apples will ripen six to ten times faster at room temperature than if they are refrigerated.

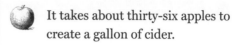
It takes about thirty-six apples to create a gallon of cider.

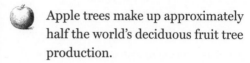
Apple trees make up approximately half the world's deciduous fruit tree production.

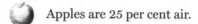
Apples are 25 per cent air.

to mid-winter. That way, they will have time to establish their root systems before what might be a dry summer and the next harsh winter. Apple trees like full sun and a warm, sheltered site that isn't subject to late frosts (which can damage the flowers). They can be grown against a wall and trained formally as cordons, espaliers or fans, but be careful that the soil at the base of the wall isn't dry. To remedy this, try digging in lots of well-rotted manure before you plant.

Some interesting facts:

Apples, peaches and raspberries are all members of the rose family.

Apple trees take four to five years to produce their first fruit.

Saving seeds

With the shortening of the days comes a slowing down of the productivity of your garden. There is lots to do, but the vibrancy of spring and summer is becoming a memory. You may have had a bountiful harvest, and your store cupboards may be bursting at the seams, but the garden is preparing to take a nap. If you have selected plants and seeds that are not hybrids, you can save the seeds for the following year. Once they have been gently dried, seeds can be stored in airtight containers for several years. We have been saving seeds and growing plants from our own seeds for five or six years now, and it's very satisfying to have established our own lines.

Hybrid plants have been produced by crossing two varieties of the same plant species to get the best qualities from each

variety. The seeds saved from these plants can be less vigorous and the resultant plants can be more variable in quality, so are not a good option to save from year to year.

Seeds should be stored in a cool, dark and dry place – and it is really important to label your treasure properly with the crop type, variety, date and any other notes you wish to make. It's also worth remembering to collect your seeds from the best plants you have grown. Unsurprisingly, some seeds store and live longer than others. For example, onion and carrot seeds are known to be very short lived, but scientists in Israel have confirmed that an ancient date palm seed retrieved from the rubble of Masada and about 2,000 years old was successfully germinated. That makes it the oldest seed ever to sprout. As a rule of thumb, most vegetable and flower seeds may be kept for one year without appreciable decrease in germination.

Lots of fruits and vegetables are mature enough to sell or are ready for eating long before the seed is mature. Examples of these include: carrots, parsnips, cucumbers, peas, green beans, summer squashes and cabbage. It is obvious really, as we want to eat tender young veggies but the plant has to mature and keep putting energy into the seeds to make them viable. So, for seed savers, you will need to leave a few plants to fully mature.

The easiest seeds to save (and germinate) are lettuce, beans or peas. One of the first crops we started growing at the Château was salad bowl lettuce. You simply harvest the leaves as they grow. At some stage, the plant will go to seed, and we found that it self-

seeded with spectacular success. So much so that we had a second crop with no work at all, and now we only collect the seeds to allow us to plant it where we want!

If you harvest your own seeds, you can easily end up with many more than you will ever need for your own garden, especially broccoli, radish or kale, all of which make excellent sprouted seeds (see further notes in the Winter section).

Our Perfect Autumn Breakfast - Cauliflower Kedgeree

SERVES
4

A complete breakfast in its own or as part of a spread.

Ingredients

½ cauliflower (about 500g/1lb 2oz), leaves and stalk removed

300g (10½oz) smoked haddock

2 tbsp vegetable oil

1 tbsp curry powder

1 onion, diced

1 tbsp chopped fresh parsley

1 tbsp chopped fresh coriander

1 spring onion, thinly sliced

4 hard-boiled eggs, shelled and halved

Methodology

1. Preheat the oven to 180°C/Fan 160°C/350°F.

2. Roughly chop the cauliflower, then blend it in a food processor until it resembles breadcrumbs. Transfer to a large baking tray and roast in the oven for 10 minutes. Stir to turn the cauliflower, then roast for a further 10 minutes until starting to brown. Remove from the oven and set aside. Season to taste.

3. Meanwhile, place the smoked haddock fillet, skin side up, in a high-sided frying pan. Add enough water to cover and bring to a gentle simmer. Cook gently for 8 minutes. Remove the haddock from the pan and set aside until cool enough to peel. Discard the skin and flake the flesh. Reserve 4 tablespoons of the cooking water.

4. Heat the oil in a large frying pan over a medium heat, add the curry powder and stir well. Add the onion and cook gently for 5 minutes, stirring until softened. Add the roasted cauliflower, smoked haddock and reserved cooking water. Season to taste. Stir gently and cook for 2 minutes.

5. Remove from the heat, stir in the fresh herbs and spring onion and transfer to a warm serving platter. Top with the boiled egg halves and serve.

Autumn Feasting

Cullen Skink

SERVES
6–8

Who doesn't love Cullen Skink or variations of this traditional soup? It is a meal in a bowl, but with a little extra effort and a fried leek garnish it can become a dinner party treat. Serve with home-made wheaten bread and butter and this is a filling meal.

Ingredients

3 leeks, trimmed and cleaned

100g (3½oz) butter

500g (1lb 2oz) potatoes, peeled and diced

1 litre (1¾ pints) vegetable stock

300g (10½oz) undyed smoked haddock, skin removed and flesh cut into 2.5cm/1-inch chunks

300ml (½ pint) single cream

sunflower oil, for frying

Methodology

1. Cut off and reserve some of the greener part of the leeks and thinly slice the white part.

2. Melt the butter in a large saucepan and add the sliced white leeks. Sprinkle in a pinch of salt and cook gently for 5 minutes over a low heat until the leeks have softened.

3. Add the potatoes and pour in the stock. Bring to the boil and simmer for 5 minutes until the leeks are soft. Add the smoked haddock and cook for 5 minutes, by which time the potato should be al dente.

4. Pour in the cream and add some white pepper. Continue to cook for a further 3–4 minutes, until the potatoes start to break down.

5. Meanwhile, take the reserved green part of the leeks and cut them in half lengthways and then into long, thin strips (like long matchsticks). Heat about 1cm (⅓ inch) of sunflower oil in a large frying pan over a high heat, add the leek strips, in batches, and fry for about 2 minutes until evenly golden and crispy. Remove with a slotted spoon and drain on some kitchen paper.

6. Divide the soup between warmed soup plates and serve with the crispy fried leeks scattered over the top and some wheaten bread on the side.

Roast Pumpkins or Squashes and Celeriac

SERVES
6

This looks lovely and is a complete meal for vegetarians. You may not use all the seeds but, as they are so yummy, keep the leftovers to nibble on!

Ingredients

1.5kg (3lb 5oz) mixed pumpkins or squashes, trimmed, halved, deseeded and cut into 2cm (¾ inch) slices

500g (1lb 2oz) celeriac, peeled and cut into 2cm (¾ inch) slices

2 tbsp extra-virgin olive oil

200g (7oz) mixed seeds and nuts (sunflower, pumpkin, pine nuts)

2 tbsp soy sauce

1 chilli, finely sliced

Methodology

1. Preheat the oven to 200°C/Fan 180°C/400°F and line a large baking tray with baking paper.

2. Toss the pumpkins or squashes and the celeriac with the oil and season well with salt and pepper. Place on the prepared tray and roast for 40–45 minutes until soft and golden.

3. Meanwhile, place the mixed seeds and nuts in a dry frying pan and toast over a medium heat, tossing frequently. When the seeds are a light brown colour, turn off the heat and pour the soy sauce over the top. Add the chilli and mix with a spatula until coated, then allow to cool completely.

4. Arrange the squashes and celeriac on a platter and scatter over the seeds and chilli to serve.

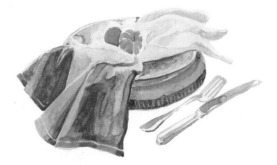

Roast Pork, Crackling, Red Cabbage and Apple

SERVES
6–8

Cold roast pork with home-made chutney is amazing so always buy a bigger joint than you need and it will cater for a couple of days. Store the raw joint in the fridge, unwrapped, as it will allow the skin to dry out and help with your crackling.

Ingredients

2–3kg (4lb 8oz–6lb 8oz) boned and rolled pork shoulder

2 tbsp olive oil

2 onions, cut into thick wedges

FOR THE CABBAGE

75g (2¾oz) butter

2 onions, diced

4 apples, peeled, cored and chopped

½ red cabbage, cored and finely shredded (approximately 1kg/2lb 4oz)

75g (2¾oz) sultanas

2 tbsp soft brown sugar

50ml (2fl oz) cider vinegar

250ml (9fl oz) vegetable stock

Methodology

1. Remove the pork from the fridge 1 hour before cooking to allow it to come up to room temperature.

2. Preheat the oven to 240°C/Fan 220°C/475°F.

3. If the pork has not already been scored by a butcher, use a very sharp knife to score the skin (this allows the fat to escape during the cooking process). Brush all over with the oil and season well with sea salt. Place the sliced onions in a roasting tin and place the pork on top (make sure the onions are tucked underneath the meat). Roast for 25 minutes, then reduce the temperature to 190°C/Fan 170°C/375°F and roast for another 25 minutes per 500g (1lb 2oz) until the skin is really crispy. Remove the pork from the oven, transfer it to a board and cover loosely with foil.

4. Meanwhile, cook the cabbage. Melt the butter in a heavy-based saucepan and fry the onions for 5 minutes over a medium heat until softened. Add the apples and cook for 3–4 minutes, then stir in the cabbage, sultanas, sugar, vinegar and stock.

FOR THE APPLE SAUCE

4 Granny Smith apples, peeled, cored and chopped

FOR THE GRAVY

3 tbsp fat from the roasting tin

2 tbsp flour

300ml (½ pint) cider

Bring to a simmer, cover with a lid and cook gently for 15–20 minutes, until the cabbage is softened. Remove the lid and turn up the heat until most of the liquid has evaporated. Remove from the heat, replace the lid and keep warm.

5. To make the apple sauce, place the apples and 4 tablespoons of water in a small saucepan and cook over a medium heat for 10–15 minutes until the apples have softened. Using a stick blender, purée to make a smooth sauce. Set aside.

6. To make the gravy, strain the roasted onions from the tin, reserving 3 tablespoons of the cooking fat. Press the cooked onions through a sieve into a saucepan. Add the reserved fat and place over a medium heat. Stir in the flour and cider and bring to the boil. Cook for 5 minutes, stirring, until the sauce is thickened. Season to taste.

7. To carve the pork, cut away and discard the string. Using a pair of kitchen scissors, cut through the crackling so the meat is easier to access. Cut the pork into thickish slices and serve with the braised cabbage, apple sauce, gravy and potatoes of your choice.

Spiced Honey Old-fashioned

Like all good cocktails, the simplicity would lead you to believe that it's easy to come up with ideas for your own cocktails, but it requires a deft touch and quality ingredients. Here, the orange peel is a must and when you have chosen your favourite whisky you will have made it your own.

Ingredients

500ml (18fl oz) water (or apple juice for the kids)

100ml (3½fl oz) clear honey, or more to taste

1 orange, thinly sliced

2 thick slices of fresh root ginger, bashed

2 cinnamon sticks, lightly bashed

4 star anise, lightly bashed

a handful of cardamom pods, bashed

2 bay leaves

2 fresh rosemary sprigs

150ml (5fl oz) whisky (for the grown-ups)

Methodology

1. Pour the water or apple juice into a saucepan and stir in the honey until dissolved. Place over a low heat and add all the remaining ingredients except for the whisky. Heat gently for 20 minutes without boiling to allow the wonderful flavours to develop and infuse.

2. Just before serving, remove the pan from the heat and pour in the whisky, if using (serve the kids' old-fashioneds straight from the pan, making sure it isn't too hot).

3. Divide between glasses so everyone gets some of the lovely aromatics.

Autumn Vases

The golden hues of autumn need to be celebrated. From the browns of foliage to the orange and pinks of dahlia blossoms, everywhere you look it's like a postcard. And I love seeing the corn and pumpkins in the garden. So why not combine the two for a beautiful autumn vase, to make an amazing centrepiece (you would not know but the dahlia is faux!).

Pumpkin

1. Choose a pumpkin the appropriate size and make sure that it sits flat without rocking or wobbling.

2. Cut off the top and scoop out the insides with a spoon.

3. Use in the same way as you would a vase.

Corn

1. Use the wire to secure the corn cobs around the outside of the pot.

2. Wrap the jute, cord or tape around the cobs to hide the wire.

3. Place on a charger plate.

4. Use in the same way as you would a vase.

You will need

PUMPKIN VASE

- Pumpkin
- Knife
- Spoon

CORN VASE

- Thin wire
- Dried sweetcorn cobs
- Plant pot or watertight container with straight sides (if using a plant pot, a watertight container that sits inside is required)
- Jute, cord or tape
- Large charger plate (to sit the pot on)

Top Tips

- Great autumn flowers include: dahlia, cotoneaster, honeysuckle berries (the black ones), hawthorn berries, hops, medlar, pyracantha and French mulberry (the purple ones).

Autumn Chandelier

A bare branch covered in lichen and dried leaves is the inspiration for this chandelier. Add some twinkly lights and autumnal colours, and you've got the perfect chandelier for your autumn table.

How to

1. Wrap the tree branch with the thin wire or artificial garland.

2. Position your hanging rail over the centre of the table. Use the thin wire or garland to attach your branch to the rail.

3. Decorate along the length of the branch, slipping dried leaves under the wire or artificial garland and using all sorts of autumn goodies.

You will need

- Small, lightweight tree branch (preferably dried but with the bark on)
- Thin wire or an artificial autumn leaf garland
- Over table hanging rail
- Dried autumn leaves (see page 224), nuts, berries, cones, etc.

Top Tips

- Choose a branch with interesting bumps and shapes, and cut it to fit the length of the table.

- We used larch cones, beech mast, hops and poppy heads as our decorations.

- When deciding what height to hang the branch, be mindful of the hanging decorations obstructing views across the table.

Apple Crêpe Flambé with Calvados Sauce

MAKES 8*

*22CM (8½INCH) CRÊPES

All over our part of France there are numerous creperies that celebrate the humble pancake. Mostly this involves spreading a crêpe with your chosen filling and then folding or rolling it prior to service. This dish follows the principles of a Crêpe Suzette and so is served with gently cooked fruit and soaked in a sugary buttery alcoholic sauce.

Ingredients

150g (5½oz) plain flour

a pinch of salt

2 eggs, beaten

300ml (½ pint) semi-skimmed milk

25g (1oz) butter, plus extra for cooking

vanilla ice cream, to serve

FOR THE CALVADOS SAUCE

3 tbsp caster sugar

250ml (9fl oz) good-quality apple juice

1 tsp lemon juice

4 tbsp Calvados (or apple brandy)

50g (1¾oz) unsalted butter, cut into small cubes

Methodology

1. To make the crêpes, sift the flour and salt into a bowl and make a well in the centre. Pour the beaten eggs into the well and start whisking slowly. Steadily pour in the milk, whisking as you gradually incorporate all the flour. Whisk until the batter is smooth. Set the batter aside to rest for 30 minutes.

2. Meanwhile, prepare the sauce. Tip the caster sugar into a large non-stick frying pan. Set over a low-medium heat. Allow the sugar to melt slowly, without stirring, and continue to cook until it becomes a light amber-coloured caramel. Immediately take the pan off the heat and add the apple juice, being careful as it may splatter and spit. Add the lemon juice and half the Calvados, then return the pan to a low heat to re-melt the caramel. Add the butter in small pieces, then heat gradually and simmer gently, stirring continuously until glossy and reduced slightly. Set aside.

3. Just before making the crêpes, melt the 25g (1oz) of butter and whisk into the rested batter.

4. Heat a 22cm (8½ inch) 'crêpe' pan over a medium heat. Very lightly grease the pan with a little butter, then pour about 75ml (2¾ fl oz) of the batter into the pan and swirl it around so the bottom of the pan is evenly coated. You want to use just enough batter to make a delicate, thin pancake. Cook the pancake for about 45 seconds, then use a palette knife to flip the pancake over and cook on the other side for about 30 seconds.

5. Place an upturned soup plate or similar bowl on a plate and slide the crêpe out of the pan and onto this dome. Cover with a clean tea towel to stop it from drying out but allowing it to breathe. Continue making crêpes and adding them to your pile, until all the batter is used.

6. Return the sauce to the heat. Add all the pancakes to the pan to warm through by placing them, one at a time, flat in the pan, then folding them into quarters in the warm sauce. Push the folded crêpe to the side to allow space for the next one. When all the crêpes are in the sauce, add the remaining Calvados and warm through for 1 minute. Using a lighter or matches, set the warm Calvados alight to flambé the crêpes.

7. Transfer to a warmed platter and serve immediately topped with vanilla ice cream.

Caution

Cold brandy does not ignite easily but when it is heated the vapour that is given off can burn impressively.

Kouign Amann

SERVES
10-12

Kouign Amann means 'butter cake' in Breton, the Celtic language of Brittany in northwest France. This is not a quick cook but, boy, is it worth it! Basically, there are three phases – make the dough, add the butter, then add the sugar.

Ingredients

FOR THE DOUGH

250g (9oz) plain bread flour, plus extra for rolling

5g (⅛oz) fresh yeast (1½ tsp dried yeast)

150ml (5fl oz) tepid water

15g (½oz) unsalted butter, melted

½ tsp fleur de sel (good-quality sea salt)

250g (9oz) unsalted butter, softened

250g (9oz) caster sugar

FOR THE CIDER ICE CREAM

250ml (9fl oz) dry cider

150g (5½oz) caster sugar

250ml (9fl oz) double cream

250ml (9fl oz) full-fat milk

¼ tsp ground cinnamon

3 large egg yolks, beaten

Methodology

1. You will need 10–12 × 10cm (4 inch) ring moulds. Start preparing several hours ahead of serving.

2. To make the cider ice cream, pour the cider into a saucepan and add the sugar. Place over a low heat and heat gently until it has dissolved. Add the double cream, milk and ground cinnamon, stir, and allow to heat gently until it just simmers. Remove from the heat and slowly whisk the egg into the hot cider liquid, beating continuously until combined. Return the liquid to the heat, stirring constantly until it has thickened a little (it will not be as thick as a regular custard, but similar to thin cream). Take off the heat and let it cool completely. Transfer to an airtight container and freeze until ready to serve.

3. To make the dough, sift the flour into a bowl and crumble in the fresh yeast, or add the dried yeast. Add the salt and tepid water and melted butter and work the mixture together to form a soft, sticky dough. Knead gently in the bowl for a minute or so, until you can shape it into a ball. Cover the bowl and leave to rise for 30 minutes at room temperature.

4. Meanwhile, place the block of unsalted butter between 2 sheets of baking paper and, using a rolling pin, tap down the block first, then roll out to make a square of flattened butter approximately 20 × 20cm (8 × 8 inches). Cover and chill for 30 minutes.

5. Transfer the rested dough to a lightly floured surface and roll out to form a thin 28cm (11 inch) square. Lay the butter in the centre at a 45-degree angle, forming a diamond. Fold the corners of the dough into the middle to form an envelope and press to seal. Cover and chill for 20 minutes.

6. Return the chilled dough to the lightly floured surface and roll out away from you to form a long, thin rectangle approximately 25 × 45cm (10 × 17¾ inches). Fold the bottom third of dough up and then the top third down and press the edges to seal. Rotate through 90 degrees and repeat the rolling and folding. Cover and chill for 30 minutes.

7. Return the chilled dough to the lightly floured surface and roll out to a rectangle again and sprinkle half the sugar over the surface, leaving a 1cm (⅓ inch) border. Fold up as before. Rotate through 90 degrees and roll out again. Sprinkle with the remaining sugar, fold as before and press to seal. Cover the dough and leave to stand at room temperature for 30 minutes. Line a large baking tray with baking paper. Arrange the metal ring moulds on the baking paper spaced slightly apart.

8. Roll out the dough a final time to a rectangle approximately 5mm (¼ inch) thick – it will be even longer than before. Using a sharp knife cut the dough into 1.5cm (½ inch) strips. Roll up the strips from the end nearest to you to form tight spirals and transfer to the moulds cut side down. Cover the tray with a tea towel and leave to rise for a final 45 minutes.

9. Preheat the oven to 180°C/Fan 160°C/350°F.

10. Transfer the tray to the oven and bake for 40 minutes until the pastries are risen and golden brown. Immediately remove the pastries from the moulds, taking care as they will be hot, or the caramel will harden. Leave them to cool slightly on a clean sheet of baking paper. These are best served still warm and with ice cream.

Wild Flower Lanterns

For many of us, crafting is an escape, a chance to be fun and creative. This craft takes me right back to my youth . . . papier mâché on a balloon. And, just between us, when Dorothy gave up, I finished these off on my own – and had an absolute ball!

You will need

- Small balloons
- Clingfilm
- Jam jars
- Parchment paper
- Wallpaper paste (or PVA)
- Paintbrush
- Dried wild flowers (see next page)
- Rubber gloves
- Scissors
- Jute/cord
- Battery-operated tea lights

How to

1. Blow up the balloons to a nice size (not too big).

2. Cover the balloons in a layer of clingfilm and twist it around the knot.

3. Place the balloons in the jam jars (knots down).

4. Rip the parchment paper into small pieces and, using the wallpaper paste or PVA and a paintbrush, cover the balloons in a thin layer of paper. Only cover three-quarters of the balloons.

5. Position the wild flowers on the balloons and cover with wallpaper paste or PVA to secure in place.

6. Cover the flowers with another layer of parchment, smoothing them with your fingers (wear rubber gloves for this bit).

7. Set aside until completely dry.

8. Slowly let the air out of the balloons.

9. Trim the dried parchment to tidy up the edges. Make a small hole in the top of both sides and thread jute/cord through to make a handle.

10. Place a battery-operated tea light in each lantern.

Top Tips

- Put a line on the balloon before you start, to indicate where to stop covering.

- Be gentle with the finished lanterns, they are very fragile.

- Only use battery-operated tea lights.

Pressing Flowers

How to

1. Cut the flowers on a dry, sunny day for best results (so the flowers themselves are at their driest and not wet with dew or rain).

2. Carefully place the flowers between sheets of blotting paper and cardboard. Layer them in this order: card, paper, flower, paper, cards etc.

3. When finished, apply pressure with a pile of books, or something heavy. Alternatively, use a flower press.

You will need

 Flowers

 Blotting paper or paper towels (not needed if using a flower press)

 Pieces of cardboard (not needed if using a flower press)

 Books, something heavy, or a flower press

Top Tips

- Spread the petals to make the flowers the best shape before pressing. You cannot change the shape after they have been pressed or they will break.

- Remove excess flowers, petals or leaves from the stem before pressing if there are any that overlap or make the flower too thick.

- Make sure the paper is untextured, or the texture will transfer to the flower.

- You can also press flowers in a book – preferably a notebook with blank pages. Place the flowers between the pages of the book. Once loaded, use a pile of books or something heavy to press the notebook shut.

Meatloaf

SERVES 4

Meatloaf has always been considered a humble meal but the flavours are amazing and served with a mustard mash and green beans it is worthy of any table.

Ingredients

2 tbsp olive oil

1 onion, diced

375g (13oz) minced beef

250g (9oz) minced veal

125g (4½oz) minced pork

12g (⅓oz) salami or ham, diced

2 carrots, grated

3 tbsp chopped fresh thyme

3 tbsp chopped fresh parsley

2 small eggs, beaten

2 garlic cloves, crushed

75g (2¾oz) fresh breadcrumbs

150ml (5fl oz) full-fat milk

2 tbsp Worcestershire sauce

150g (5½oz) rashers of rindless streaky bacon

FOR THE GLAZE

100ml (3½fl oz) tomato ketchup

50ml (2fl oz) orange juice

2 tbsp soft brown sugar

2 tbsp Worcestershire sauce

1 tbsp hot sauce (optional)

Methodology

1. Preheat the oven to 180°C/Fan 160°C/350°F. Line a 900g (2lb) loaf tin with clingfilm, pressing down well into the corners. Set aside.

2. Heat the olive oil in a small saucepan over a low heat. Add the onion and fry gently for 5 minutes, until soft. Remove from the pan and leave to cool.

3. In a large bowl mix together the beef, veal, pork, salami or ham, carrots, herbs, eggs, garlic, breadcrumbs, milk and Worcestershire sauce. Add the cooled onion and season with salt and pepper. Stir really well until evenly combined.

4. Take the rashers of streaky bacon and very carefully press into the loaf tin, slightly overlapping and allowing the ends to hang over the rim. Spoon the meat mixture into the tin, pressing down firmly. Fold the ends of the bacon over the meat filling to conceal it. Flip the 'loaf' out onto a baking tray, remove the tin, then the clingfilm and bake in the middle of the oven for 50–60 minutes, until a knife slipped into the centre comes out hot to the touch.

5. A few minutes before the meatloaf is ready, place all the glaze ingredients into a saucepan and heat gently over a low heat, stirring to dissolve the sugar. Bring to the boil, then remove from the heat.

6. Remove the meatloaf from the oven and pour the glaze over the top. Serve in slices.

Duck Parmentier

SERVES 6

Think a rich and unctuous shepherd's pie but made with duck.

Ingredients

1 onion, diced

2 carrots, diced

1 celery stick, diced

1 garlic clove, finely chopped

1 tbsp plain flour

300ml (½ pint) dry red wine

4 × 250g (9oz) confit duck legs, skinned, boned and flesh diced, plus 2-3tbsp duck fat from the legs

1kg (2lb 3oz) large potatoes, peeled and cut into chunks

100ml (3½fl oz) double cream

Methodology

1. Preheat the oven to 200°C/Fan 180°C/400°F. Lightly oil 6 × 250ml (9fl oz) ramekins or individual baking dishes.

2. Heat the duck fat (taken from the confit legs, if possible) in a large frying pan over a low heat. Add the onion, carrots and celery and fry gently for 10 minutes until really soft. Add the garlic and cook for 30 seconds, then stir in the flour and cook for 1 minute.

3. Pour in the wine and stir until smooth. Increase the heat and bring to the boil. Stir in the duck meat and cook for 1 minute. Remove from the heat and divide the mixture between the prepared ramekins.

4. Meanwhile, boil the potatoes for 15 minutes or until completely tender. Drain them well, then return them to the pan to dry briefly over a low heat. Pass the potatoes through a ricer (or use a masher) and stir in the cream. Season with salt and pepper.

5. Spoon or pipe the potato on top of the duck in the ramekins and fluff up the surface with a fork. Place all the ramekins on a baking tray and cook in the oven for 20–25 minutes until the topping is golden and the filling is bubbling nicely.

Pumpkin Napkin Rings

Many years ago, I was gifted an 'Angel' pin cushion. It took pride of place in my trésorerie and has gone on to inspire many similar crafts. Here I've turned the pin cushion design into a napkin ring. Making a stuffed ball of felt is a simple but very effective technique – once you've mastered it, you will be wondering how else you can use it.

You will need

 Scissors

 10–15cm (4-6 inches) of gold, bronze or orange (autumnal colours) felt or fabric (use offcuts if you can)

 Strong (or double strand) cotton

 Needle

 Small amount of Dacron or cotton wool for stuffing

 Gold thread (or your chosen colour)

 Small pieces of green felt

 Hot glue gun

 Glue sticks

 Green pipe cleaners (one for each pumpkin you intend to make)

How to

1. Cut a circle out of the autumn-coloured felt or fabric with a diameter of 9cm (3½ inches).

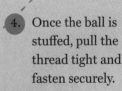

2. Using strong (or double strand) thread, sew a line of running stitches around the circumference of the circle, approximately 0.5cm (¼ inch) from the edge. Don't cut or tie the thread when you have completed the circle.

3. Pull the thread to create a puff. Fill the felt or fabric with a little stuffing to create a ball.

4. Once the ball is stuffed, pull the thread tight and fasten securely.

5. To create a pumpkin shape, use the gold thread (or your chosen colour) and sew through the centre of the bottom of the ball and come up out of the top. Go back into the centre of the bottom, so the thread rests against the ball, and pull the thread out through the top again. Pull slightly to indent. Repeat to make multiple segments. I like to go down the opposite side, gradually make the segments smaller, but you can decide as you go! When you have made 8 segments, tie off the thread.

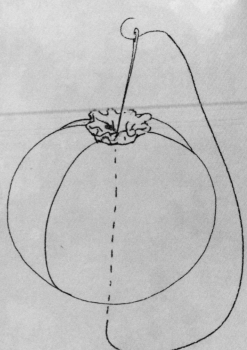

6. Cut out a circle from the green felt with a diameter of 2.5cm (1 inch).

7. Using the hot glue, stick the green felt circle to the top of the pumpkin to hide the gathered material.

8. Using the hot glue again, stick a pipe cleaner in place on top of this circle to make a stalk. I like the look of 2 pumpkins together. Wrap the pumpkin(s) around a napkin to create a ring.

Fig Tart

SERVES 8

When we have lots of figs we are always looking for different things to do with them!

Ingredients

ready-made sweet pastry case

100g (3½oz) unsalted butter, softened

100g (3½oz) golden caster sugar

2 eggs

1 tsp vanilla extract

150g (5½oz) ground almonds

pinch of salt

4 tbsp fig jam

12 figs, quartered lengthways to look like teardrops

Methodology

1. Preheat the oven to 180°C/Fan 160°C/350°F and make a ring of foil 2.5cm (1 inch) wide with a length to fit the circumference of the tart case. Place the ready-made sweet pastry case in the freezer for 10 minutes to ensure it is firm.

2. Meanwhile, place the butter in a bowl and beat with an electric whisk until it is creamy. Add the sugar and mix again. Add the eggs and vanilla extract and mix for a third time. Stir in the almonds and salt and mix well.

3. Remove the pastry case from the freezer and spread the base with the fig jam. Pour the batter into the tart case and level the surface. Arrange the fig pieces on top.

4. Place the tart in the oven to cook for 35 minutes. Remove from the oven and press the foil loosely over the outer edge of the crust of the pastry case to protect it, then continue to bake for a further 20–25 minutes. Allow to cool slightly before serving.

Autumn Crumble with Calvados Cream

SERVES
6–8

Bramleys are at their best in the autumn, and are crying out to be made into pies or crumbles.

Ingredients

FOR THE CRUMBLE

250g (9oz) wholemeal flour

¼ tsp ground nutmeg

¼ tsp ground cinnamon

125g (4½oz) butter, cubed

125g (4½oz) soft brown sugar

FOR THE APPLES

75g (2¾oz) golden sultanas

200ml (7fl oz) apple juice

50g (1¾oz) butter

50g (1¾oz) caster sugar

½ cinnamon stick

4 Bramley apples, peeled, cored and chopped into thick wedges

25ml (1fl oz) Calvados (or apple brandy)

FOR THE CALVADOS CREAM

250ml (9fl oz) double cream

25ml (1fl oz) Calvados (or apple brandy)

Methodology

1. Preheat the oven to 200°C/Fan 180°C/400°F. To make the crumble, combine the flour and spices together in a mixing bowl. Add the butter and, using your fingers, rub in to create a breadcrumb consistency. Stir in the sugar. Spread the crumble mixture over a baking tray and cook in the oven for 12–15 minutes, stirring halfway through, until lightly golden. Remove from the oven and set aside.

2. Meanwhile, place the sultanas in a bowl and add 50ml (2fl oz) of the apple juice. Leave to soak until required.

3. Place the butter, sugar, remaining apple juice and cinnamon in a saucepan over a low heat, until the sugar is dissolved and the butter melted. Increase the heat and boil for about 10 minutes, until a buttery caramel.

4. Stir in half the Bramley apples, lower the heat and simmer for 10–15 minutes until the apples are softened. Remove from the heat and discard the cinnamon stick. Strain the sultanas and stir them into the apple mixture with the Calvados. Stir in the remaining apple slices.

5. Spoon the apple mixture into a crumble dish. Spread the crumble mixture over the top and bake for 30–35 minutes, until the sauce is bubbling around the sides. Cover the dish with foil if the top starts to look too brown.

6. Just before serving, make the Calvados cream. Whip the double cream to firm peaks, then fold through the Calvados. Serve alongside the crumble.

Autumn Walk

Hot Chocolate Spoons

SERVES 2

There are many shortcuts to making hot chocolate but, to be honest, if you take to many shortcuts, you have to compromise on the flavour. Time makes it tastier!

Ingredients

a little sunflower oil, for greasing

150g (5½oz) dark, white or milk chocolate (as preferred)

a handful of mini marshmallows and/or chocolate buttons, to decorate

450ml (18fl oz) full-fat milk

100ml (3½fl oz) single cream

a little whipped cream, to serve

a tot of rum (for the grown-ups)

You will need egg cups and small teaspoons.

Stop before you feel sick!

Methodology

1. Brush the egg cups with oil (be sparing here).

2. Roughly chop 100g (3½oz) of the chocolate, then melt it in a microwave or in a bowl over a pan of just simmering water, making sure the bowl does not touch the surface of the water. Divide the melted chocolate between the oiled egg cups and top each one with some marshmallows, chocolate buttons or a combination of both. Set aside for about 30 minutes to cool but not set. Once cool, press a teaspoon into the middle of each chocolate egg cup, then leave to set completely.

3. Grate the remaining 50g (1¾oz) of chocolate and set aside.

4. Once the chocolate egg cups are set, dip them in hot water for about 1 minute, to release the chocolate from the cups. Pull gently on the spoons and, as soon as they are out of the cups, roll them in the grated chocolate. Reserve the remaining grated chocolate for serving. Set aside.

5. When ready to serve, place a chocolate spoon into each mug or cup.

6. Pour the milk and cream into a saucepan and place over a medium heat. Bring to the boil, then pour immediately into the mugs or cups. Stir the spoons until the chocolate melts into the hot milk and makes a wonderfully rich and delicious hot chocolate. Top each mug or cup with some whipped cream, a sprinkling of grated chocolate and a tot of rum for the grown-ups.

Bonfire Night

Potimarron Soup with Whipped Cream

If you grow these squash, you can store them in a cool place all the way through to spring.

Ingredients

1 potimarron squash (approximately 1.5–2kg/3lb 5oz–4lb 8oz)

750ml (1⅓ pints) good chicken stock

400ml (14fl oz) double cream

juice of ½ lemon

2 tbsp light soy sauce

oil, for frying

6 large dollops of whipped cream (you can use leftovers from above) or use an aerosol of whipped cream

> **Caution**
> Every squash ie different, so be prepared to balance the saltiness and lemon to make it work for you.

Methodology

1. Peel the potimarron, reserving some of the skin for decoration. Scoop out and discard the seeds. Cube the flesh and place it in a large saucepan with the stock. Bring to the boil, then reduce the heat and simmer for 30–35 minutes until softened.

2. Add the double cream, lemon juice and soy sauce. Remove the pan from the heat and, using a stick blender or a food processor, blend into a creamy soup. Return to the heat and adjust seasoning as required.

3. Meanwhile, to crisp the squash skin, heat a shallow layer of oil in a small frying pan over a high heat. When hot, add the skin and fry for about 30–40 seconds until crisp and golden. Drain on kitchen paper.

4. Serve the soup in cups, glasses or bowls and top with a dollop of whipped cream and the crispy skin pieces.

Spicy Western Beans

SERVES 6–8

Spicy beans should be different every time!

Ingredients

2 tbsp olive oil

2 onions, diced

4 garlic cloves, finely chopped

1 red chilli, deseeded and finely chopped

350ml (12fl oz) orange juice

225ml (8fl oz) passata

8 tbsp golden caster sugar

4 tbsp Maggi or Worcestershire sauce

6 × 400g cans of beans, drained and rinsed (we use a mix of kidney, flageolet and haricot)

Methodology

1. Heat the oil in a large flameproof casserole dish over a medium heat. Add the onions and fry gently for 5 minutes. Add the garlic and chilli and cook for 30 seconds.

2. Stir in the orange juice, passata, sugar and Maggi or Worcestershire sauce, increase the heat and bring to the boil.

3. Stir in the beans and return to a simmer. Cover the pan with a lid, reduce the heat and cook for 20 minutes. Remove the lid and cook for a further 5 minutes, until thickened and glorious.

4. Keep warm until ready to serve.

They will give you gas!

Caution

Hasselback Potatoes

SERVES
6

These are to be cooked in thick (or double-layered) foil at the edge of your bonfire, in the oven or in a Dutch oven on the fire. It's all about the cutting . . . I get Arthur to prepare these so he can hone his knife skills.

Ingredients

6 large or 12 medium baking potatoes

2 tbsp olive oil

lots of butter, to serve

Methodology

1. Preheat the oven to 200°C/180°C fan/390°F.

2. To prepare the potatoes, place them on a chopping board and cut deep slits across the potatoes without cutting all the way through. (You could place a chopstick, spatula or wooden spoon on each side of the potato as a 'stop' or 'guide' so, as you slice down, the knife will cut only as far as the stops or guides allow.) Keep your cuts straight, close together and equally spaced to make the potatoes beautiful. Finally, cut a single slit down the length of the potato (perpendicular to your other cuts), rub all over and into the slits with the oil and season with sea salt. Place the potatoes on a roasting tin and bake in the oven for 45–50 minutes, depending on the size of your spuds, until cooked.

3. When cooked, squeeze the sides to open your cuts and add in a piece of butter that is twice as big as you think it should be. Serve with the Spicy Western Beans (see page 218).

Chunky Scarf

My nan loved to knit. She would sit for hours every day and I was always fascinated with the patterns she could create. I never had quite the same patience but I promise this arm-knitted scarf is easy and so much fun to make. It's also guaranteed to bring the wow factor!

You will need

- Super super chunky wool (I used 2 balls, but it depends how long you want the scarves)
- Scissors
- 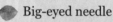 Big-eyed needle

How to

1. When you knit using your arms, you transfer the stitches from one arm to the other. That means that if you cast onto your right arm, you will transfer the stitches over to your left arm by the end of the first row. And then, back to your right arm at the end of the second row.

2. Start by making a slipknot – make a loop in the wool and then pull a second loop of wool through this. Slip this second loop onto your right arm. This will be your first cast on stitch.

3. Continue to loop the wool and pull loops through to create more cast on stitches. Slip these stitches onto your arm as you go. Continue casting on until you have 6 stitches.

4. To knit the first row, take the free end of the wool and hold it in your right hand (set the tail at the end of the first cast on stitch aside). Then, still holding the wool pull the first loop on your right arm over your hand. As you pull the loop through, slide the old loop off your right arm and slide the new loop (now in your hand) onto your left arm. Continue to knit the stitches in this way until you reach the end of the first row.

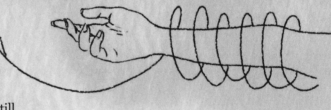

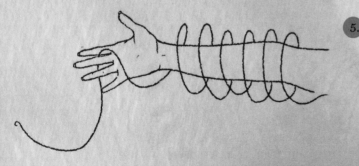

5. Repeat this process, moving the stitches from your left to your right arm. In other words, hold the wool in your left hand and pull the first loop on your left arm over your hand then place the loop now formed in your left hand onto your right arm etc.

6. When the scarf is as long as you want it, you will need to cast off. Finish with the stitches on your left arm. To cast off, knit the first 2 loops in your row, then, stop knitting. Take the first loop on your right arm and pull this loop up and over the second loop on your right arm. You should now only have one loop on your right arm. Knit the next stitch from your left arm onto your right and repeat the casting off.

7. When there is only one loop left on your right arm, cut the wool and pull the free end of wool through this loop.

8. Using a big-eyed needle, weave the tail end of the wool through the loops on the edge of the scarf to hide it.

Warm Cider with Calvados

SERVES
6-8

Autumnal colours and the rich bounty of apples inspire this drink. You have to make this recipe your own, with your preferred cider, your chosen mix of spices and apples and the apple cider you love the most.

Ingredients

2 x 75ml (2¾fl oz) bottles of sweet cider

125ml (4fl oz) Calvados (or apple brandy)

3 tbsp soft brown sugar

2–3 cinnamon sticks, bashed (plus a few extra to decorate)

finely grated zest of 1 orange

finely grated zest of 1 lemon

Methodology

1. Measure the cider, Calvados, brown sugar, bashed cinnamon sticks and half the orange and lemon zest into a saucepan. Place over a medium heat and bring to the boil, stirring, then reduce the heat and simmer very gently for just 2 minutes.

2. Remove from the heat and leave to cool for 10–15 minutes.

3. Strain the cider into glasses and divide the remaining orange and lemon zest between them. Serve warm with a cinnamon stick to stir.

Leaf Jars

You can't beat an autumnal walk – the crunching leaves and the beautiful colours of the trees. This is an easy and rustic craft that requires just a couple of recycled jars and some of nature's free gifts. These jars add a lovely warm glow to any autumn evening gathering.

Dried Leaves

1. Pick a variety of leaves on a dry day.

2. Leave them to dry naturally overnight.

3. If the leaves curl, iron them on a low heat (without steam) between 2 sheets of parchment paper.

How to

1. Using a paintbrush, cover the jars with a liberal coating of PVA glue.

2. Position the dried leaves on the jars and cover them with a layer of PVA glue.

3. Leave to dry.

4. Pop a tea light in the bottom of the jar.

5. Finish the jars with some jute/cord tied around the neck.

You will need

- Leaves
- Iron
- Ironing board
- Parchment paper
- Small paintbrush
- Selection of jars/ nice vases
- PVA glue
- Tea lights
- Jute or cord

Top Tips

- Choose leaves with interesting shapes, like acers.

- It works nicely if you put the front (or right side) of the leaf against the glass with the back side of the leaf (the wrong side) outermost, especially if it is a waxy leaf like laurel or holly.

- Revisit the leaves now and then as the glue is drying, to make sure they are flat against the glass.

Toffee Apples – Pommes d'Amour Rouge

We always have a couple of spare apples so no 'toffee' is wasted. However, it's just a fact that the last one will never be covered properly and so eating it is officially the 'chef's perk'. In our case, when I felt there wasn't going to be enough for another whole apple, I popped two bits of apple in the pan, then onto a plate for Arthur and Dorothy.

Ingredients

10–12 small red apples, stalks removed and wiped clean

10–12 lollipop sticks or equivalent

500g (1lb 2oz) caster sugar

1 tsp lemon juice

4 tbsp golden syrup

a good dash of red food colouring

Methodology

1. Line a baking tray with baking paper. Push the lollipop sticks into the stalk ends of the apples and set aside on the prepared tray.

2. Measure the sugar into a heavy-based saucepan and add 75ml (2¾fl oz) of water and the lemon juice. Place over a very low heat to dissolve the sugar. As soon as the sugar has softened and begun to dissolve, you can lift the pan slightly and swirl it around gently. Don't stir the pan as that may allow crystals to form on the sides which will spoil the texture. Once the sugar has fully dissolved, add the golden syrup. Swirl the pan to mix. Boil the sugar mixture until it reaches 149°C/300°F on a sugar thermometer and turns a golden brown colour. Alternatively, you can test whether it is ready by dropping a small amount of the caramel from a teaspoon into a glass of cold water – if it goes hard, it is ready. (Be prepared to do this a couple of times if you have children!) Immediately add the red colouring, swirling the pan until it is evenly coloured.

3. To coat the apples, hold them by the sticks and dip them into the caramel, tipping your pan so the caramel can cover the apples completely. Carefully place the dipped apples back on the lined baking tray and leave to cool and harden. They will be crunchy in a matter of moments.

Winter

Winter's rhythm is like no other. The days are shorter and colder, which gives us a great excuse to light the fire, snuggle up and watch a movie. And our cuisine changes, too; it is richer and warming.

With the winter solstice comes the start of winter and very soon afterwards the magic of Christmas.

December is steeped with tradition. Old and new. That's the thing about tradition, you can navigate it to pick the best bits that work for you! We have started lots of new traditions since moving to France – from the boys' annual oyster-foraging trip to Brittany and three generations of girls picking foliage in the garden, to Arthur and Dick making Berawecka and crafting together with the children. All of these are traditions we have created as a family since moving to the Château. Christmas is Dick's favourite time of the year and eating mince pies while we decorate the tree and argue about the lights will always be a seasonal highlight for us. It's a magical time that's all about giving, which sometimes means giving a bit of time to yourself to capture memories, so don't forget to enjoy the preparations!

December at the Château is indulgent and often packed full of celebrations. There are moments when we have no rest; but it's also the best of times, as we enjoy special moments with loved ones and laugh until our bellies hurt. We burn the candles at both ends and then love the comfort that the new year brings with fresh optimism and new opportunities.

days may be getting longer as the new year comes around, but January doesn't usually get any positive press, as it's thought of as miserable, damp and invariably cold. Our Saxon forefathers called it 'wolf month' for its unsympathetic nature. Nowadays, part of the problem may be that the next holiday is months away, so all that can be seen is winter stretching out in front of us and no one ever really knows what date Easter will be. Forget that! We think January is a lovely time to hunker down and snuggle with the heating on and log burners going. Above all else, this is our time for planning, though you can't deny that daylight is in short supply, so it is also the time to enjoy the fruits of last year's labour. Raid the *rumtopf*!

February is the coldest month of the year and we can almost guarantee our moat will freeze. However, it's also a month to look forward to positively, as the geese start laying and we have the treat of dippy goose eggs for breakfast! There are also lots of winter vegetables still in the garden, so broths and stews are on the menu. And it is a great time for fish and shellfish. The old saying was only eat oysters during months with an 'r' in them, as the oysters are exposed to higher temperatures in warmer months that allow potentially hazardous pathogens to grow.

We are so very aware that winters can feel hard, but it is worth remembering that it's also a season that changes quickly, from being the gloomiest time of year, to those days when the wintery sun is a sign of what is to come. Before you know it, the daffodils and crocuses are joined by the magnificent magnolia and the cherry blossom. And then, very soon, you realise you have started going outside without your winter woollies on and nature is truly awakening.

'*The flowers of late winter and early spring occupy places in our hearts well out of proportion to their size.*'

Gertrude S. Wister

Contents

Christmas Dinner

Festive Party

Principles of Pruning

Without doubt, pruning is an essential gardening skill. Cutting back maintains healthy looking, prolific, beautiful trees, shrubs and perennials, and the regular pruning of certain trees can increase vigour, improve fruit or flower production, and ward off disease.

Put simply, your pruning should address the four 'Ds' - the dead, the diseased, the damaged and, the most subjective, the disorderly, branches. When pruning, there are lots of principles but no rules. But for guidance:

- You should cut just above a node (where leaves, buds and shoots emerge from the stem), as this prevents 'die back' and therefore disease
- The cut should be at an angle sloping down and away from the node
- It is best not to:
  - leave too long a stem above the bud as this can rot and allow disease to get into the rest of the healthy stem
  - make a flat cut as moisture does not run off the cut, again causing rot
  - cut too close to the bud as it can restrict its food source
  - use blunt or dirty secateurs

The correct time of year to prune varies from plant to plant, but most plants are pruned in winter when dormant, though there are exceptions (cherry and plum trees, for example, are susceptible to silver laf disease and should therefore be pruned in summer when the risk of infection is reduced. Pruning at the wrong time shouldn't kill a plant, although continually doing so might weaken or damage it. In general, the worst time to prune is immediately after new shoots appear in early spring or in early autumn, as this may encourage late growth, which will be unable to withstand winter weather. Sometimes pruning at the 'wrong' time is unavoidable as it is best to prune damaged stems immediately.

Rhubarb

The rhubarb we have in our walled garden was given to us by our mate Steve, who is a builder and was given the original crown by his grandfather. Steve's grandfather had reared it in the Rhubarb Triangle, north of his hometown of Barnsley. Rhubarb is native to Siberia and thrives in the wet, cold winters of Yorkshire, where they once produced 90 per cent of the world's winter forced rhubarb (see below) in the forcing sheds that were common across the fields there. Our rhubarb established very quickly and every year it has provided us with enough for crumbles, liqueurs, syllabubs and sauces. Rhubarb does need a little space, but it earns its place in your garden, especially as any gardener you know will probably be pleased to split one of their crowns and share it with you for free.

Rhubarb is a hardy perennial that lives for many years and thrives in even the coldest sites. It's low maintenance and extremely easy to grow, but will form a large, leafy clump 1.5m (5 feet) wide or more. The top growth dies down over winter, re-sprouting every spring. Some initial patience is required, as you shouldn't really harvest any stems in the first year after planting, and only a few in the second, to allow the plant to get well established. In the third year, you can harvest normally, taking up to a third of the stalks at any one time. The leaf stalks are best picked during spring and early summer, but plants can be 'forced' in late winter by covering with a forcing jar or bucket – this manipulates the temperature and light to artificially speed up a plant's growth, flowering or fruiting.

The process of forcing rhubarb is relatively simple. If your rhubarb plant spends time in the sun, it stores energy in the crowns as carbohydrates. If they are then grown without light, and preferably with a little heat, the stored carbohydrate in the roots is transformed into glucose, which gives forced rhubarb its sour-sweet flavour. It is possible to buy large terracotta jars to place over the plants in winter to produce an early crop of delicious, blanched stems. As we have three large crowns side by side, we built a large coffin-like structure to enclose the plants. We pack it with manure and straw in the autumn, then harvest the rhubarb at the end of the winter. After our first harvest of sweet, forced rhubarb, we take the enclosure off and allow photosynthesis to put more energy into our plants.

Some interesting facts:

 Rhubarb is actually a vegetable – in fact, it is part of the polygonaceae family, which includes buckwheat and sorrel.

 It was originally found in Asia around 2,700 BC, where it was used for medicinal purposes.

 It made its way west after it was discovered by Marco Polo in the 13th century.

 The leaves of the rhubarb plant are poisonous to humans because of a high concentration of oxalic acid, which can lead to kidney stones or even organ failure if you eat too much.

Kale

Kale is one of the most nutrient-dense foods you can eat – it's packed with vitamins A, C, E, K and B6, as well as iron, folate, manganese, calcium, copper and more. Indeed, gram for gram, kale contains more vitamin C than oranges! It might now be the hot new thing, but the name kale originates from northern Middle English 'cale' (in German the equivalent word is kohl), which was a term used for various cabbages. In other words, kale has been around for a very long time, and I love the fact that it is from the family of 'wild cabbages'. If you've tried it before but found it bitter, wait until late autumn/winter and give it another go, because the taste actually gets milder when it is colder outside.

Kale is easy to grow and will thrive almost anywhere – in a garden, in a window box or in a pot. You can plant seeds or seedlings, which are widely available in garden centres. There are lots of varieties with different flavours and looks. I'm a fan of the old-fashioned curly or Siberian kale, though we grow Russian kale and cavolo nero as well. Sow or plant out in spring and you can harvest through the autumn and winter. Kale plants like the sun but will grow in light shade. And, as you'd expect from a plant with bountiful foliage, it likes rich soil. It is traditionally grown in a seed bed before being transferred to the main plot (use multi-purpose compost and plant the seeds about 1cm/½ inch deep in small pots or modules). Keep in mind that the plants will take up a lot of space when mature, so they should be planted about 46cm/18 inches apart. The leaves are ready to pick approximately fifty-five to seventy-five days from sowing, or when the leaves are about the size of your hand. The central rosette is the tastiest part of the plant, but you can use it as a 'cut and come again' crop by picking the outer leaves and letting it grow to produce more.

Potatoes

Potatoes were one of the first crops we planted in our walled garden to 'break up the ground'. It hadn't been cultivated for the best part of forty years, so I didn't bother to dig a trench and put some well-rotted manure in (as I'd been taught as a youngster). Instead, after a very coarse weeding session, we rotavated a long bed and gently popped in and covered seed potatoes every 46cm (18 inches), and that kept us in potatoes all summer long.

Being from Northern Ireland, I love good potatoes, and to teach Angela and the children what I meant, and to reinforce Arthur and Dorothy's Irish-ness, we ate our

first crop straight from the ground. I set up a small rocket stove in the garden, then, as I turned over each of the heads with my 'grape', the children collected our treasure, including the absolutely tiny, Dorothy-sized ones, and popped them into a bucket of water. When potatoes are that fresh, all you have to do is rub them in your hands and the skin and mud comes off. We gave them a quick rinse, then cooked them in boiling water for fifteen to twenty minutes. They were drained and a ridiculously large knob of butter was added. A bit of a bash and a turn later, rather than a mash, and we were each served a plate of buttery, sweet potato, completely unadulterated. They were magnificent and anyone who tries them like this will find they have discovered their new favourite dish.

As a rule of thumb, we try to get our potatoes in the ground on or around St Patrick's Day, 17 March, which is the very end of winter. That way, they are ready to start harvesting here on Bastille Day, 14 July.

But the magic of growing your own potatoes starts mid-winter, at the beginning of February. When you have chosen your seed potatoes, they need to be 'chitted', or sprouted; this helps you get an earlier, more bountiful harvest. We have some rather old chitting trays that we picked up at a car boot sale years ago, and they add to the annual ceremony. The potatoes are placed on trays in a single layer with the 'rose' (i.e. the end with the most eyes/sprouts on it) uppermost. The trays are then stored in a cool, frost-free area with moderate light (not direct sunlight). We use our potting shed.

Sprouts will appear in a couple of weeks, but planting should be delayed until mid-March, by which time the sprouts should be a couple of inches long and dark. You will know if you are storing them too warm or with the wrong amount of light, as you will end up with long, thin sprouts.

Some interesting facts:

- Potatoes originated in Peru thousands of years ago.

- They were the first food ever to be grown in space.

- They are made up of roots, tubers, stems and leaves – the bits we eat are the tubers.

Sprouting seeds

There are not many plants that you can decide to grow on a Monday and get to eat on a Sunday. And, as if that wasn't good enough, you can also sprout your own seeds in the depths of winter. If you have not tried eating sprouted seeds, you should give them a go. The sprouting process helps release enzymes which, when eaten, allow us to absorb minerals. Germination also makes digesting proteins and fats easier, so your body doesn't have to work as hard to break down and absorb what you eat. Sprouted seeds and greens also have more vitamin C, vitamin B and antioxidants that materialise at higher concentrations. Vary what sprouts you eat to ensure you get a variety of nutrients. Sprouts are high in proteins and fibre, too. But a little warning, the fibre may make it difficult to digest for some people and can cause flatulence!

The following are great seeds for sprouting: mung beans, alfalfa, broccoli, radish, kale, sunflower, pumpkin, whole lentils and chickpeas.

You can buy special jars for sprouting seeds, but all you really need is a jam jar with a piece of muslin over the opening. The first step is to soak two heaped tablespoons of your chosen seed mixture (more if the seeds are larger) in water overnight. Then drain and rinse the seeds in fresh water. Leave them in the jar with the cover loosely in place. Repeat rinsing and draining every day for approximately five days until your sprouts are ready to eat. They can benefit from a couple more days sprouting but if you keep them sprouting for too long, they will start producing chlorophyl, turning green and will become less palatable. Fear not, when they are ready to eat, they will keep in an airtight container in the fridge for several days.

As well as using sprouted seeds in salads, we love a sandwich of home-made hummus and sprouted seeds. I once sprouted too many chickpeas and, after several back-to-back sprouted chickpea meals, I decided to plant the remaining seeds and we ended up with an amazing harvest that was lovely and crunchy when fresh, and the excess we dried and used for planting the following season. You can see how easy it is to get caught in a chickpea loop!

Our Perfect Winter Breakfast – Fungi, Crème Fraîche, Thyme and Sherry on Sourdough

Describing this as 'mushrooms on toast' simply doesn't do this dish credit. You can use chestnut mushrooms or whatever selection of fungi you can get, but the addition of crème fraîche, sherry and thyme takes this dish to a new level. When the sauce soaks into the toast and softens there is even more contrast with that and the hard, sourdough crust.

Ingredients

20g (¾oz) mixed dried fungi (optional)

50g (1¾oz) butter

500g (1lb 2oz) mixed fresh mushrooms (the more variety the better), sliced

1 garlic clove, crushed

1 tbsp fresh thyme leaves

50ml (2fl oz) sweet sherry

250ml (9fl oz) crème fraîche

4 slices of sourdough (approximately 1.5cm / ½ inch) thick, chargrilled not toasted

Methodology

1. If using dried mushrooms, soak them in boiling water for 30 minutes until rehydrated. Strain, discarding the liquid, then chop the mushrooms. Set aside.

2. Melt the butter in a large frying pan over a low heat. Add the fresh mushrooms and cook for 3 minutes, shaking the pan occasionally. Add the garlic and thyme and cook for a further 1–2 minutes, until the mushrooms are lightly golden and softened.

3. Stir in the sherry and rehydrated mushrooms, if using. Turn up the heat and allow the alcohol to burn off. Add the crème fraîche and stir until it starts to bubble.

4. Season well with salt and pepper and serve immediately on the slices of chargrilled sourdough.

Christmas Table Setting

We like to go all out for our Christmas table setting: personalised place settings, lots of candles and a sprinkle of festive magic. I don't need much of an excuse to create a hanging chandelier, but at Christmas it's even more invaluable because it leaves you with plenty of room still on the table. Below are some of my ideas, but be creative and make it your own!

Christmas Chandelier

1. Position your hanging rail over the centre of the table.

2. Wrap the set of battery lights around the branch.

3. Use the ribbon/cord/string to suspend various Christmas decorations from the branch at different heights.

4. Add dried flowers, grasses and herbs for extra interest.

You will need

- Over table hanging rail
- Set of battery lights
- Small tree branch (preferably dried, with the bark stripped and cleaned)
- Ribbon/cord/string
- Christmas tree decorations
- Dried flowers/grasses/herbs
- Stepladder

Personalised Place Settings

1. Use a craft knife and cutting board to cut a piece of card to 8 × 7cm (3¼ × 2¾ inches).

2. Score down the middle of the card and fold in half.

3. Cut another piece of card to 2.5 × 7cm (1 × 2¾ inches).

4. Glue this onto the front of the folded card.

5. Use a posh pen and fancy writing to add the guests' names.

6. Pop the card into a pine cone.

You will need

- Craft knife
- Cutting board
- Card
- Paper glue
- Posh pen and nice handwriting!
- Small pine cones

Christmas Jar Fun

Many years ago, I bought the most beautiful Victorian owl enclosed in a thin parlour dome from a dealer in East London. I've always loved the curiosity of seeing wild and wonderful creatures perched inside a dome or cloche – and you can brilliantly recreate this for yourself using candles, a collection of toy animals and some glass bowls or jars.

1: Christmas Scene

1. Place the moss in the bottom of the glass containers.

2. Add small Christmas ornaments to create Christmas scenes.

2: Polar Bear

1. Turn the bowl upside down. Melt some wax candles and pour it down the sides and over the top of the bowl.

2. While the wax is still wet, push candles in so they are secure.

3. When the wax dries, create your Christmas scene and top with the bowl.

3: Simple Candle/Vignette

1. Put the candle in the holder, if using, and place in the bottom of the bowl. Cover the base with moss, hiding the holder, if using.

2. You could also decorate the bowl with small animals or Christmas tree ornaments, instead of adding a candle, if preferred.

VARIATION ONE:

You will need

- Candles
- Moss
- Glass jars, domes or bowls
- Small Christmas ornaments, like animals, deer, trees, houses

VARIATION TWO:

You will need

- Flat-bottomed bowl
- Candles
- Moss
- Small Christmas ornaments, like animals, deer, trees, houses

VARIATION THREE:

You will need

- Candle or small Christmas ornaments, like animals, deer, trees, houses
- Candle holder
- A fancy glass bowl
- Moss

Boned and Stuffed Bird

SERVES
8

(WITH LEFTOVERS)

The first question must be why go to all the effort of boning a bird? It is a fiddly job and it takes practice but, in the end, you have a 'casing' that allows you to fill the bird with your choice of stuffing and, of course, carving could not be easier, with the resulting slices being a mix of meat and stuffing. Small birds, in particular, can benefit from stuffing to keep them moist and make them go further. The forcemeat stuffing I use here, based on sausage meat, is very simple.

Ingredients

10kg (22lb) bird (turkey or chicken)

12 rashers of streaky bacon

FOR THE STUFFING

2kg (4lb 8oz) sausagemeat

Zest and juice of 3 lemons

500g (1lb 2oz) fresh breadcrumbs

9 tbsp chopped fresh parsley

Methodology

1. Place all the stuffing ingredients in a bowl. Season with plenty of salt and black pepper and mix well. If the bird has its liver and giblets, you can chop the liver and add this to the stuffing, too. Chill the stuffing in the fridge until ready to use.

2. To bone the bird, begin by removing the wingtips. Set them aside, together with the other bones when they are removed, to make stock. Slip your fingers under the skin at the neck hole, and work the skin back until you expose one of the shoulder joints. Using your knife, cut through the shoulder joint to separate the wing bones from the carcass. Repeat the process with the other wing.

3. Pull the skin a little further back over the breast, to expose the wishbone. Once you have exposed the upper part of the breast, use your sharpest knife to cut under and along the wishbone to free it of the breast meat. Remove the wishbone and add it to the stock pile.

4. Place the bird breast-side down, remove the parson's nose and cut the skin from there to the hip joint of the leg. With the point of the knife, separate the hip joint. You are now ready to trim the meat from the carcass. With the breast-side down, cut down in long, gentle slices. Keep the blade near the ribs, pushing the chicken or turkey flesh back as you go; the effect will be rather like turning a sock inside

out. Be careful during this phase to keep the blade of the knife pointed towards the carcass and be particularly careful when you get to the top of the breastbone, lest you inadvertently puncture the skin.

5. When you have done both sides, hold the carcass and allow the meat to hang below. Cut horizontally to separate the carcass from the meat – don't cut the skin!

6. Now, time for the legs. Grasp the thigh bone at the hip end and start to separate the meat from the thigh. Scrape the meat off the thigh bone. At this stage you can cut off the thigh bone, leaving the drumstick in, or continue stripping back the meat and taking out both the bones. Cut off the end of the leg. If we are roasting a stuffed, boned bird, we tend to leave the bones in the wings and drumsticks, as the final dish when presented at the table looks very like a normal roasted bird. And ever since Arthur's first Christmas, he has had a drumstick as part of his Christmas traditions, though they no longer dwarf him!

7. Finally, take the boned meat and skin and reform it back into the shape of the bird.

8. To stuff the bird, it is easiest to put it breast-side down and place your stuffing on the breast meat and push the stuffing into the thigh cavities. Then pull the edges of the skin together and either sew them or weave a skewer through the skin to join it together.

9. If you have decided not to even attempt the boning (shame on you!), to stuff your bird, gently push your fingers up under the skin of the breast from the neck end. When the skin is loose, push the stuffing in so it covers about half the breast and then fill the large flap of skin with the remainder. Turn the bird over and use a skewer to hold the flap of skin to the base of the bird.

10. Smear the bird with butter. Most people have their own family secret approach to ensuring the perfect roast turkey. As the birds are bigger, the breast meat needs to be protected, so we always cover the bird with a layer of streaky bacon over the butter and loosely place foil over the bird until the last stages of cooking when it can be allowed to brown. All weights need to include the stuffing too! For smaller birds up to 6kg (12lb 12oz) they are best cooked like chicken on a higher heat for a shorter period of time. Preheat the oven to 190°C/Fan 170°C/375°F and allow about 10 minutes per pound. For larger birds preheat the oven to 165°C/Fan 145°C/329°F and allow 20 minutes per 500g (1lb 2oz). Baste several times during the cooking.

11. Once the bird has roasted, leave it to rest as you finish all the side dishes. Do not stress about leaving a turkey for 45 minutes while you roast the potatoes in the oven; we cover our turkey in foil and set a couple of tea towels over it and it really benefits from the rest!

Sprouts, Potatoes, Crispy Kale and Bread Sauce

There are so many sides that are wonderful with roast turkey. Here are just some examples that we love.

Ingredients

FOR THE BREAD SAUCE

500ml (18fl oz) full-fat milk

2 bay leaves

large knob of butter

½ onion, spiked with 8 cloves

250g (9oz) fresh breadcrumbs

FOR THE ROAST POTATOES

100ml (3½fl oz) olive oil

1.5kg (3lb 5oz) floury potatoes, pre-boiled and left to dry

FOR THE CRISPY KALE

200g (7oz) curly kale, stalks removed and finely sliced

1 tbsp olive oil

2 tbsp demerara sugar

Methodology

1. To make the bread sauce, place the milk, bay leaves, butter and the onion/cloves in a saucepan over a medium heat. Bring it to a simmer and cook for a couple of minutes. Remove from the heat and leave to cool. Take out the onion and bay leaves, then stir in the breadcrumbs. Reheat the sauce when required.

2. When the bird comes out of the oven, increase the oven temperature to 200°C/Fan 180°C/400°F. Pour the olive oil into an oven tray and place in the oven to heat. The potatoes need to be kept in a sieve after they have been boiled and roughened up, this it to ensure they are dry before going into the oil. When the oil is hot, put the oven tray on the stove over a high heat and add the potatoes. Turn and coat them in the hot oil. Sprinkle them liberally with sea salt and place the tray on the top shelf of the oven. Cook for about 25 minutes, then give them a shake or turn the potatoes and continue to cook for a further 20 minutes.

FOR THE SPROUTS

200g (7oz) lardons

6 small shallots, peeled but left whole

3 garlic cloves, peeled but left whole

800g (1lb 12oz) Brussels sprouts, peeled

250ml (9fl oz) chicken stock

12 sweet chestnuts

FOR THE CARROTS

25g (1oz) butter

6 carrots, peeled and cut into chunks

300ml (½ pint) stock

300g (10½oz) frozen peas

3. Place the kale on a baking tray and drizzle over the olive oil. Sprinkle with the sugar and season with sea salt and black pepper. Toss well so everything is coated. Roast in the oven for the last 15 minutes of the potato cooking time, tossing halfway through, until it is crispy.

4. Meanwhile, put the lardons in a cold saucepan, and place them over a low heat. When the fat is rendered out, add the shallots and garlic cloves. Sauté for 3–4 minutes, then add the sprouts and stock, cover with a lid, and simmer for 5 minutes. Remove the lid, add the chestnuts and continue cooking until all the stock has evaporated. Remove from the heat and cover with a lid until ready to serve.

5. Melt the butter in a pan and sauté the peeled and cut carrots gently for 3–4 minutes. Add the stock then bring to a simmer for another 3–4 minutes. You can then add the frozen peas and when it comes back to a simmer for a minute they are ready. Strain and serve. The cooking liquid can be added to your gravy if you wish to add a little sweetness.

Pork Stuffed Cabbage

SERVES 8

When you've cooked the cabbage, use the stock to make a thick gravy. This is great served with potato purée.

Ingredients

1 Savoy cabbage (about 1kg/2lb 4oz)

2 tbsp olive oil

75g (2¾oz) bacon lardons

1 onion, diced

1 garlic clove, crushed

600g (1lb 5oz) minced pork

150g (5½oz) fresh breadcrumbs

2 tbsp chopped fresh parsley

1 egg, beaten

500ml (18fl oz) boiling chicken stock

Methodology

1. Preheat the oven to 200°C/Fan 180°C/400°F. Remove any torn outer leaves from the cabbage and discard. Trim the base so it sits flat, but be careful not to cut too close to the base of the leaves.

2. Bring a large saucepan of water to the boil, add the whole cabbage and return to the boil. Cook for 5 minutes then remove the cabbage from the pan. Refresh under cold water, then set aside to drain and dry thoroughly.

3. Place the cabbage on its stalk end and gently peel back the outer 5–6 layers of leaves, revealing the rounded heart in the middle. Carefully pop a knife under the heart and cut through the stalk close to the base to remove it, without cutting through the outer leaves. (Reserve the heart to be used separately.)

4. Meanwhile, place the olive oil in a frying pan over a medium heat. Add the lardons and onion and fry for 3–4 minutes. Stir in the garlic and cook for a further 1 minute. Set aside to cool completely.

5. Put the onion mixture in a large bowl and add the pork, breadcrumbs, parsley, egg and plenty of salt and white pepper. Mix together thoroughly then form into a ball. Press the ball into the hollowed-out cabbage and draw the outer leaves back over the meat to enclose it. Transfer the stuffed cabbage to an ovenproof casserole dish and pour in the boiling stock. Cover the pan with a lid and bake in the oven for 50–55 minutes until the internal temperature is 74°C/165°F or a skewer inserted into the centre of the cabbage comes out piping hot. Serve by cutting into segments.

Christmas Filo Nests with White Sauce

SERVES
6

A variation on Christmas pudding, and the sweet crispy filo adds another texture.

Ingredients

12 sheets of filo pastry

50g (1¾oz) butter, melted

icing sugar, for dusting

1 ready-made Christmas pudding

FOR THE WHITE SAUCE

50g (1¾oz) margarine (definitely not butter!)

50g (1¾oz) plain flour

300ml (½ pint) full-fat milk

2 tbsp sugar

Methodology

1. Preheat the oven to 180°C/Fan 160°C/350°F. Grease an 8-hole muffin tray including the horizontal bits between the holes.

2. Cut each sheet of filo into 20cm (8 inch) squares, then cut each square into 2 triangles. Brush a triangle of filo with melted butter, then lay it in one of the muffin holes, gently pushing it down into the base and against the sides. (You can use a little ball of leftover pastry to do this, as it would be gentler than fingers.) Dust the pastry with a little icing sugar. Brush another triangle of filo with melted butter and lay it over the top, in the same muffin hole but at a 60-degree angle to the first. Gently push it into the base again and dust with a little icing sugar. Repeat with a third piece of pastry. You should now have a delicate filo bowl with pointy bits sticking out. Repeat to make one per person and a couple of spares (they are delicate).

3. Place the muffin tin in the oven and bake for 10–15 minutes until the pastry is golden brown. Remove from the oven and leave the pastries to cool in the tin.

4. Meanwhile, to make the white sauce, place the margarine and flour in a saucepan over a low heat and cook for 1–2 minutes. Add the milk slowly, stirring all the time. When it starts to thicken, stir in the sugar.

5. Heat the Christmas pudding as instructed and put the warm sauce in a jug. To assemble the puddings, use an ice-cream scoop to scoop a ball of pudding into each nest. Dust with icing sugar.

Festive Wreaths

It's become a Château tradition for me, mum and Dorothy to forage in the garden for foliage, mistletoe and pine cones. Three generations, three pairs of secateurs! Making a garland is a great seasonal craft everyone can enjoy for very little expense. Dorothy made her first wreath at six years old, and Dick and I once enjoyed a festive wreath-off! (I won, but who's counting . . . ?)

How to

1. Make small bunches of mixed foliage and tie them together with florist tape or thin wire.

2. Secure in place on the wreath frame with cable ties, working around the wreath and overlapping as you go, so it looks full.

3. Decorate with dried oranges/fruits and golden walnuts (see below).

Dried Oranges/Fruits

1. Cut the fruits into rings about 0.5cm (¼ inch) thick (3mm / ⅛ inch for apples and pears).

2. Lay the fruit in a single layer on a tray.

3. Dehydrate via your preferred method:

4. Dehydrator/oven

5. Dry for approximately 6–12 hours at 40–60°C (104–140°F). (If you increase the temperature to 65°C / 150°F, it decreases the drying time but will also discolour the fruits a little.)

You will need

- Lots of foliage (we use laurel, conifer, eucalyptus, holly, ivy and mistletoe)
- Florist tape or thin wire
- A wreath frame – any circle (in our case a big hula hoop that splits into two)
- Cable ties
- Dried oranges/fruits and golden walnuts (see below)

You will need

- Cutting board
- Oranges/lemons/ limes/apples/pears
- Thin wire
- Knife (a mandolin is better for the apples and pears, as very thin slices are required)
- Desiccator/ dehydrator/air fryer/ oven

Top Tips

The air needs to circulate around the fruit, so the fruit should be in a single layer with space between each piece.

Golden Walnuts

1. Screw an eyelet into the bottom of each walnut.

2. Hold the walnut at the opposite end to the screw eyelet and spray the eyelet end gold.

3. Repeat with all the walnuts.

4. Pierce a small cardboard box with multiple slits and use these to hold the nuts.

You will need

- Walnuts
- As many screw eyelets as you have walnuts
- Gold spray paint
- Small cardboard box
- Thin wire

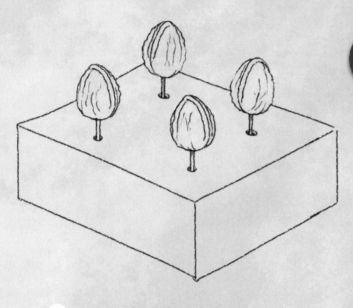

Top Tips

- Use a high gloss spray paint.
- Spray two to three layers of paint for a metallic finish.

5. With the nuts held in the box, eyelet side down, spray the rest of them with the gold paint.

6. Leave them to dry.

7. Add some wire to each eyelet and use this to attach the walnuts to the wreath.

Winter Broth

SERVES 8

We use beef for our broth but you could use lamb (scrag end is perfect). We grow red celery that is not widely available in shops but it is perfect for broth if you can source it. Our broth mix is a combination of dried pearl barley, yellow split peas, green split peas, whole dried peas and red split lentils. Usually this would be soaked before use but I prefer a 'second-day' broth so it does not need to be pre-soaked.

Ingredients

500g (1lb 2oz) beef shin (in a single slice with the bone)

2 tbsp olive oil

1 leek, trimmed, cleaned, halved lengthways and cut into 5mm (¼inch) slices

2 carrots, diced

3 celery sticks, diced

150g (5½oz) broth mix (see Introduction)

3 litres (5⅓ pints) beef stock

200g (7oz) kale, thinly sliced

Methodology

1. Rub the beef shin with a little of the olive oil and season with salt and pepper. Heat a large saucepan over a high heat and sear the shin for 2–3 minutes a side until browned. Remove with a slotted spoon and set aside.

2. Lower the heat and add the remaining oil to the pan. Stir in the leek, carrots and celery and fry for 2–3 minutes. Add the broth mix, stir once, then return the beef to the pan.

3. Pour in the stock and bring to the boil. Leave the broth to simmer for at least an hour, skimming any congealed protein (called scum) off the top.

4. Once the vegetables, beef and broth mix are cooked, adjust the seasoning to taste – do not be shy with the pepper. Stir in the kale, remove the pan from the heat and set aside to cool. Leave in the fridge overnight.

5. The following day, remove the beef from the broth and cut the flesh into small pieces, discarding the bone. Return the meat to the pan and bring the broth to a simmer.

6. Serve with wholemeal bread.

Beef Stew with Red Wine and Dumplings

SERVES
6–8

The red wine takes the sauce here to a different level. However, the little superstars here are the dumplings that should be fluffy, light, crispy on top and soft below.

Ingredients

FOR THE STEW

3 tbsp olive oil

1kg (2lb 4oz) boneless beef shin, cut into 3cm (1¼ inch) cubes

250g (9oz) bacon lardons

500g (1lb 2oz) small shallots, peeled but left whole

250ml (9fl oz) tomato passata

1 tbsp tomato purée

500ml (18fl oz) red wine

500ml (18fl oz) beef stock

FOR THE DUMPLINGS

150g (5½oz) beef suet

400g (14oz) self-raising flour

1 tbsp chopped fresh rosemary

½ tsp salt

½ tsp ground white pepper

Methodology

1. Preheat the oven to 170°C/Fan 150°C/338°F. Heat 1 tablespoon of oil in a flameproof casserole dish over a high heat and brown the beef, in batches, for 5 minutes, adding more oil, if necessary. Remove from the pan with a slotted spoon and set aside.

2. Add any remaining oil to the dish with the lardons and fry for 2–3 minutes until browned. Reduce the heat to low, add the shallots and cook for 5 minutes until they start to soften. Return the beef to the pan along with the remaining stew ingredients. Bring to the boil, cover with a lid and transfer to the oven. Cook for 2 hours until the beef is tender.

3. About 10 minutes before the stew is ready, make the dumplings. Combine the suet, flour, rosemary, salt and white pepper in a bowl. Add 150–160ml (5–5½fl oz) of cold water to form a soft, sticky dough. The dumplings should be spiky and not smooth when formed.

4. Remove the dish from the oven and increase the oven temperature to 200°C/Fan 180°C/400°F. Take large spoonfuls of the dumpling mixture and drop them onto the surface of the stew. Return the dish to the oven and cook, uncovered, for 25–30 minutes until the dumplings are fluffy with crunchy tops and soft bottoms. Serve with winter greens.

Beef and Mushroom Puff Pastry Pie

SERVES
6

Great served with kale. Tying the herbs in with a bit of butchers' twine produces a bouquet garni that makes the whole dish more aromatic.

Ingredients

20g (¾oz) dried mushrooms

500ml (18fl oz) hot beef stock

300ml (½ pint) brown ale

1kg (2lb 4oz) braising steak, cubed and dried with kitchen roll before cooking

5 tbsp olive oil

2 onions, diced

a bouquet garni made with thyme, rosemary and bay

1 tbsp Maggi or Worcestershire sauce

250g (9oz) chestnut mushrooms, halved

50g (1¾oz) butter, softened

3 tbsp plain flour

250g (9oz) ready-rolled puff pastry

1 egg, beaten

Methodology

1. Preheat the oven to 170°C/Fan 150°C/338°F.

2. Put the dried mushrooms in a jug with the hot beef stock and set aside to soak for 20 minutes. Remove the mushrooms, then roughly chop them and set aside. Add the ale to the stock in the jug and set aside.

3. Season the beef. Heat 2 tablespoons of the olive oil in a flameproof casserole dish over a high heat and brown the beef in batches for 4–5 minutes until browned. Remove the beef with a slotted spoon and turn down the heat to low.

4. Add a little more oil to the pan and stir in the onions. Fry gently for 5–6 minutes until softened. Return the beef to the dish with any beef juices, the rehydrated mushrooms and the stock mixture. Add the bouquet garni and the Maggi or Worcestershire sauce and bring to a simmer. Cover the dish with a lid and transfer to the oven. Cook for 2 hours until the beef is very tender.

5. Just before the beef is ready, heat the remaining oil in a large frying pan and fry the chestnut mushrooms over a high heat for 3–4 minutes until browned. Meanwhile, stir the softened butter and plain flour together to form a smooth paste.

6. Remove the casserole dish from the oven and discard the bouquet garni. Stir in the chestnut mushrooms. Dot the butter and flour paste over the surface of the stew and stir gently until it has melted into the sauce and caused it to thicken. Leave the stew to cool to room temperature.

7. Increase the oven temperature to 200°C/Fan 180°C/400°F.

8. Taste the stew and season if you think it needs it. Spoon the stew into a 2 litre (3½ pint) pie dish. Carefully unroll the sheet of pastry and lay it across the top of the pie. Trim off the excess pastry with a sharp knife and flute the edges. Brush the top with the beaten egg and bake in the oven for 40–45 minutes until the pastry is golden.

9. Leave to sit for 10 minutes before serving.

Festive Sloe Gin Cocktail

SERVES
1

Traditionally, sloes need to be harvested after the first frost, however, if you leave it too long the birds (or other sloe gin makers) can get there before you. Like many things, time enhances the pleasure, and when you open your first bottle it's always an excuse for a party.

Ingredients

1 shot of sloe gin

2 shots of Campari

ice cubes

crémant or club soda

a slice of lemon, to decorate

a few blueberries or sloes (if available), to decorate

Methodology

1. Put the gin and Campari into a shaker with some ice cubes and shake well.

2. Strain into a glass and top up with either crémant or club soda.

3. Decorate with a lemon slice and some sloes or blueberries, if available.

Lemon Meringue Roulade

SERVES 8–10

Back home in Northern Ireland, my sister always makes a couple of pavlovas at this time of year to make a change from the heavy Christmas desserts. Just to be clear, this is no attempt to reduce calories! We love this at the Château as our 'light' pudding.

Ingredients

5 egg whites

275g (9¾oz) caster sugar

50g (1¾oz) flaked almonds

400ml (14fl oz) double cream

zest of ½ lemon

6 tbsp lemon curd

icing sugar, for dusting

Methodology

1. Preheat the oven to 200°C/Fan 180°C/400°F. Grease and line a 23 × 33cm (9 × 13 inch) Swiss roll tin with baking paper.

2. In a large, clean bowl, whisk the egg whites with an electric whisk on full speed until very stiff. Keep whisking at full speed as you gradually add the caster sugar, a tablespoonful at a time, whisking well between each addition. Continue whisking until all the sugar is incorporated and the mixture is extremely stiff and glossy.

3. Spread the meringue evenly over the base of the prepared tin and sprinkle over the almonds. Bake in the oven for 12 minutes, or until golden. Lower the temperature to 180°C/Fan 160°C/350°F and bake for a further 20 minutes until firm to the touch. Loosely cover the surface with foil if it becomes overly brown.

4. Remove the meringue from the oven and turn it out, almond-side-down onto a clean sheet of baking paper. Remove the baking paper from the base and leave the meringue until cool to the touch.

5. Whip the cream until it forms stiff peaks, then fold in the lemon zest and half the lemon curd. Spread the lemon cream evenly over the cold meringue. Drizzle the remaining lemon curd over the cream right up to the edges. Roll up the meringue from one narrow end to form a roulade. Dust with icing sugar and serve in slices.

Trifle with Summer Jam

SERVES 8–10

Trifle is a wonderful blend of fruit, custard, sponge, alcohol and cream. It is possible to make every element from scratch or you can buy ready-made products to assemble the trifle in the final dish.

Ingredients

500ml (18fl oz) jelly (your chosen flavour)

250g (9oz) sponge fingers (or sliced Madeira cake)

100g (3¾oz) strawberry jam

75ml (2½fl oz) sweet sherry, masala, crème de cassis or your preferred sweet liqueur

500g (1lb 2oz) frozen summer fruits, defrosted

500ml (18fl oz) double cream

grated milk chocolate, to decorate

FOR THE CUSTARD

300ml (½ pint) full-fat milk

200ml (7fl oz) single cream

2 egg yolks

2 tbsp cornflour

50g (1¾oz) caster sugar

½ tsp vanilla extract

Methodology

1. Make the jelly according to the packet instructions and leave it to cool but not set.

2. To make the custard, place the milk and single cream in a large saucepan over a low heat and heat gently until just below boiling point. Meanwhile, in a large bowl, whisk the yolks, cornflour, caster sugar and vanilla until smooth. Gradually pour the hot milk into the yolk mixture, whisking constantly. Return the custard to the pan and heat gently, stirring constantly, until it thickens. Remove from the heat, place clingfilm on top to prevent a skin forming and set aside to cool. Chill until required.

3. Assemble your trifle. Line your trifle bowl with sponge fingers, then spread the jam haphazardly over the top in dollops. The objective is to not do it uniformly. Drizzle the sherry or other liqueur over the top.

4. Spoon the defrosted summer fruits (and juice) over the sponge layer, then pour on the cool jelly. Transfer to the fridge and leave to firm up and set. Once the jelly layer is set, spoon the cooled custard over the top.

5. Whip the cream to firm peaks, then spoon over the custard. Dust with grated chocolate to serve.

Custard Cups

We were given a collection of beautiful Edwardian custard cups by Dick's mum. They are gorgeous and delicate and so we set about developing a warm, light custard and 'mildly' alcoholic drink that was suitable to be taken pre-dinner or after a chilly walk in the country.

Ingredients

250ml (9fl oz) full-fat milk

200ml (7fl oz) single cream

½ vanilla pod, split

3 egg yolks

60g (2¼oz) caster sugar

freshly grated nutmeg

a good splash of brandy, to serve

Methodology

1. Place the milk, cream and vanilla pod in a saucepan over a medium heat until it just reaches boiling point. Remove from the heat and set aside to infuse for 15 minutes. Discard the vanilla pod, scraping the seeds into the milk.

2. Beat the egg yolks and sugar together in a large bowl until pale. Stir in the infused milk, then return the mixture to the saucepan and place over a low heat. Stir for 5–6 minutes, until the custard thickens to just coat the back of a wooden spoon. Do not allow the custard to boil or it will spoil.

3. Pour in brandy to taste and divide between teacups or glasses. Place a star template over each cup and dust lightly with some ground nutmeg.

Festive Party

Oysters Two Ways

SERVES
10–12

We are lucky enough to be able to go to the coast and collect our own oysters. They are a traditional Christmas Eve canapé in France, but not everyone loves a raw oyster, so we serve some of ours cooked and even non-oyster-eaters love them!

Ingredients

24 oysters (size 3)

½ garlic clove, crushed

50g (1¾oz) fresh breadcrumbs

lemon wedges, to serve (optional)

FOR THE BECHAMEL

50g (1¾oz) butter

20g (¾oz) plain flour

150ml (5fl oz) full-fat milk

½ tbsp chopped fresh chives or parsley

FOR THE MIGNONETTE

2 tbsp red wine vinegar

1 shallot, finely chopped

Methodology

1. Start with the shucking. Fold an old tea towel over 4 or 5 times to make a nest for holding the oyster. Always shuck with the 'bowl' half of the oyster on the bottom, as you want to save as much of the liquid as possible. (It is also worth noting that oysters must be stored with the bowl at the bottom to keep them in the best possible condition.) Starting from the hinge end, work your oyster knife (or strong, short-bladed knife) into the hinge. This is the part that takes practice, but it's not about brute force. Wiggle the knife tip around until you feel it going in between the top and bottom shells, then you can exert some pressure against both by twisting and prying them apart. Once you have done that, slide the blade between the two shells, keeping it as flat as you can against the top shell. Approximately two-thirds of the way through is where the anchor muscle is, so just sweep the knife across until you sever it. Once you cut the muscle, you should be able to pull the top shell off. Arrange the meat neatly in the liquid in the bottom shell and move onto the next oyster.

2. Make a bechamel by melting half the butter in a small saucepan over a medium heat. Add the flour and stir until combined. Allow to cook for 1 minute, then gradually beat in the milk and continue to stir as it comes to the boil. Cook for 1 minute. Take off the heat and set aside to cool. Stir in the fresh herbs and a pinch of salt.

3. Preheat the grill to medium.

4. Melt the remaining butter in a frying pan over a medium heat. Add the garlic and cook gently for 30 seconds to soften. Remove the pan from the heat and add the breadcrumbs and a pinch of salt. Stir until well coated.

5. Arrange 12 oysters on the grill tray (or pop them in a muffin tray so they sit flat) and put a teaspoon of bechamel on each oyster. Sprinkle a good layer of breadcrumbs on top of the bechamel, then place the oysters under the grill for approximately 5 minutes, or until the sauce is bubbling and the breadcrumbs are golden.

6. For the remaining 12 oysters, arrange them on a plate and make the mignonette. Combine the vinegar with the shallot in a small bowl. Season with cracked black pepper and spoon a little onto each oyster.

7. Serve the cooked oysters with lemon wedges and the raw oysters at once.

Crispy Lingot with Chilli Honey Dip

MAKES 15–20

Lingot is a soft, Camembert-like cheese made within a kilometre of the Château and is Arthur's favourite cheese. We developed this canapé for Grandma and Papi Steve's fiftieth wedding anniversary.

Ingredients

100g (3½oz) plain flour

3 eggs, beaten

150g (5½oz) dried breadcrumbs (panko work well)

2 Lingot cheeses, cut into 'fingers' or wedges

vegetable oil, for deep-frying (or a spray oil for an air fryer)

125ml (4fl oz) runny honey

1 small red chilli, deseeded and finely chopped

Caution

If you do not completely cover the fingers with the egg they will not seal and your gooey cheese will escape.

Methodology

1. Place the flour, eggs and breadcrumbs in separate shallow bowls (large enough to fit the fingers of cheese). One at a time, dip the cheese fingers into the flour, shaking off the excess, then into the beaten egg, making sure it is covered, then allow the excess egg to drip off before finally dipping into the breadcrumbs. Roll the cheese until it is evenly and completely coated in the breadcrumbs. Repeat with all the cheese fingers.

2. To deep-fry, heat about 5cm (2 inches) of vegetable oil in a deep-fat fryer or heavy-based saucepan until it reaches 170°C/338°F on a sugar thermometer. As soon as the oil is up to temperature, add the crumbed cheese fingers in batches of 3–4 and fry for about 2 minutes until golden and crispy. Remove carefully with a slotted spoon and place on kitchen paper to absorb the excess oil. Repeat with all the cheese fingers.

3. Meanwhile, warm the honey and chilli in a small saucepan over a low heat, then set aside.

4. Place the chilli-infused honey in dipping bowls and serve with the cheese fingers.

Scallops in a Boat

MAKES
24

It's all about decadence.

Ingredients

200g (7oz) scallops (white meat only), plus 2–3 extra to garnish

1 egg white

zest of ½ lemon

2 tbsp double cream

24 × 4cm (1½ inch) ready-made mini pastry shells

1 tbsp vegetable oil, seasoned

Methodology

1. Preheat the oven to 190°C/Fan 170°C/375°F.

2. Place the scallops in a food processor and pulse 5 or 6 times until they are coarsely chopped. Add the egg white and pulse until well combined, scraping down the sides as required. Add the lemon zest, a pinch of sea salt, a good pinch of white pepper and pulse until incorporated. Finally, slowly pour in the cream while the processor is running. Scrape down the sides to make sure everything is mixed evenly, then blend again, if necessary.

3. Transfer the scallop mousse to a piping bag with a plain nozzle and pipe it into the pastry shells.

4. Thinly slice the extra scallops, toss in the seasoned vegetable oil and divide between the pastry cases, on top of the mousse. Transfer the shells to a baking tray and bake in the oven for 5–6 minutes until the mousse is set.

5. Serve warm.

Photo Booth

It doesn't take much to convince our friends and family to pose for a photo but, nonetheless, adding a fancy frame to your party also helps give everyone the confidence to be that extra bit fabulous! It can be as simple as a painted old picture frame, a door frame decorated with fabric, or a curtain covered in balloons.

How to

1. Blow up the round balloons to different sizes.

2. Attach the back cloth to the frame using either glue dots or carpet tape.

3. Fasten the larger balloons into clusters using the long modelling balloons as string and tie them onto the frame.

4. Use any smaller balloons to fill in the gaps. Attach them in place with the glue dots or carpet tape.

You will need

- Balloons – lots of them, in your choice of colours and shapes, make sure you've got some round ones

- Long balloons – the type used for balloon modelling

- Back cloth to fit the frame

- Large frame to mount the balloons (a clothes rail works a treat or see introduction for more ideas)

- Double-sided glue dots or carpet tape

Top Tips

- You'll need lots of puff or you could buy a £12-machine to do the blowing up for you – honestly, it's worth the investment!

- The back cloth can be super sparkly (like mine!), or as plain as you wish.

- My balloons had a metallic finish for that extra Christmassy look!

- Make sure you have different-sized balloons.

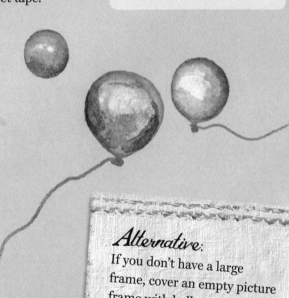

Alternative:
If you don't have a large frame, cover an empty picture frame with balloons and ask guests to hold this in front of themselves for a picture.

Savoury Mince Pies

SERVES 8

Arthur and I worked on this recipe together and it was a great success, so we have them every year. And another tradition was born! We call them coffin pies because of their rectangular shape.

Ingredients

FOR THE PASTRY

100g (3½oz) lard

4 tbsp full-fat milk

450g (1lb) plain flour

2 tsp salt

icing sugar, to dust

FOR THE MINCEMEAT

700g (1lb 9oz) lean beef or mutton mince

100g (3½oz) beef suet

½ tsp ground cloves

½ tsp ground black pepper

½ tsp ground mace

a pinch of saffron

a good pinch of salt

50g (1¾oz) raisins

50g (1¾oz) currants

50g (1¾oz) pitted prunes, chopped

Methodology

1. Preheat the oven to 200°C/Fan 180°C/400°F. You will need 8 × mini loaf tins.

2. Combine all the mincemeat ingredients in a large bowl and mix together until evenly combined. Set aside.

3. To make the pastry, place the lard, milk and 150ml (5fl oz) of water in a saucepan over a medium heat, until the lard melts, then bring to the boil. Remove from the heat, add the flour and salt in one go and beat thoroughly with a wooden spoon until completely mixed. Tip the dough out onto a lightly floured surface and knead until smooth – I get Arthur to do this but wait until the dough has cooled slightly!

4. Divide the dough into two-thirds and one-third. Cover the smaller piece and keep warm. Divide the large piece into 8 and roll out each piece to a thin (about 2mm / ¹⁄₁₆ inch) rectangle about twice the size of the tins. Repeat with all 8 pieces. Carefully manoeuvre the pastry into the tins, making sure you get it well into the sides. Cut off any overhanging pastry, then transfer the tins to a large baking tray.

5. Spoon the mincemeat into the pastry cases, pressing down well.

6. Divide the remaining pastry into 8 and roll out each piece to be a little bit larger than the top of the tins. Dampen the edges of the pastry with water then top the pies, pressing down around the rim to seal. Crimp the edges and make a couple of small slits in the centre of each pie.

7. Bake in the oven for 25–30 minutes until the pies are golden and the filling is piping hot. Remove from the oven and cool in the tins for 5 minutes, then carefully remove and leave to cool on a wire rack.

8. Serve at room temperature and dust with a little icing sugar.

Home-made Gifts

You cannot beat the feeling of receiving a home-made gift and, for me, the fun of sitting down with Arthur and Dorothy to create our presents is all part of the excitement of the season. Warning: The pride on the children's faces when they see someone open their gift will melt your heart!

Air-dry Clay O and X Game

1. Roll out the clay to a 5mm (¼ inch) thickness and cut a 10 × 10cm (4 × 4 inch) square.

2. Using a fork (or something similar) mark the board to create a 3 × 3 grid (i.e. 9 squares).

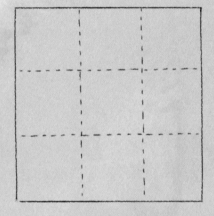

3. Use your fingers to mould a lip around the edge of the square.

4. Roll out some more clay and use the O and X cutters to make 5 of each.

5. Leave everything to dry on parchment paper.

6. When it is dry, sand any edges smooth, if necessary, and paint, if desired.

Pebble and Fabric O and X Game

1. Paint the pebbles – 5 with Os and 5 with Xs.

2. Cut a piece of fabric 11 × 11cm (4¼ inches).

3. Hem all 4 edges with a 0.5cm (¼ inch) seam.

4. Sew 2 lines horizontally and 2 vertically to create a 3 x 3 grid.

O and X Game Bag

1. Cut the patterned fabric into a 22cm (8½ inch) square.

2. With the right side down, fold the top 7cm (2¾ inches) over in half to create the channel. Pin in place.

You will need

- Scrap patterned fabric
- Scissors
- Sewing machine
- Cotton
- Pins
- 40cm (16 inches) of cord

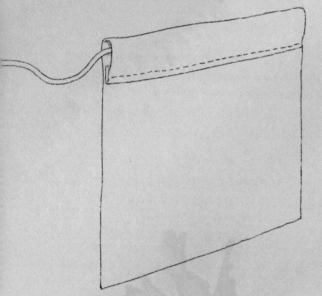

3. Thread a cord through this channel, then sew in place, being careful not to go through the cord.

4. Fold in half lengthways (right sides together) and sew down the long edge, starting below the channel, and along the bottom edge with 0.5cm ((¼ inch) seams. Turn the bag inside out.

Top Tips

For an extra bit of fun, sew the grid onto the front of the bag before you sew the bag, that way it will never be misplaced.

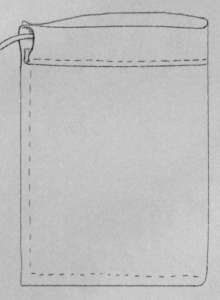

Leftover Turkey 'Stars'

SERVES 12

It's the law to buy a turkey that is bigger than you actually need, so this is an alternative to turkey pie, turkey vol-au-vents, turkey curry and turkey soup!

Ingredients

350g (12oz) ready-made shortcrust pastry

200g (7oz) leftover turkey meat, roughly chopped

100g (3½oz) leftover stuffing, roughly chopped

4 tbsp cranberry or redcurrant jelly

1 egg, beaten

a few sesame or nigella seeds, to garnish

Methodology

1. Preheat the oven to 180°C/Fan 160°C/350°F.

2. Divide the pastry into 12 equal pieces and roll out each piece on a lightly floured surface until 2mm (¹⁄₁₆ inch) thick. Cut each piece into a 10cm (4 inch) square, then make a cut diagonally about a quarter of the way towards the opposite corner.

3. Place the turkey meat and stuffing in a food processor and blend until you have a fairly smooth paste. Divide into 12 equal-sized balls and flatten a little to make small patties.

4. Spread 1 teaspoon of jelly in the middle of each pastry square and pop a turkey patty on top. Draw the corners of the pastry up into the centre, overlapping them, and press firmly together to seal. This will give you your star shape (as in the picture).

5. Brush each pastry with a little beaten egg and sprinkle some sesame or nigella seeds over the top. Place the pastries on a lined baking tray and bake in the oven for 15–20 minutes until golden.

6. Transfer to a wire rack to cool slightly, but serve while still warm.

Berawecka

This very sweet and moreish cake keeps well and can be enjoyed throughout the festive period. It also makes a lovely present. We cook it in a number of different ways – shaped into an oval and slightly flattened like a bread, then baked on a buttered baking sheet, or cooked in miniature buttered bread tins to make neat rectangles.

Ingredients

250g (9oz) dried pear

250g (9oz) dried apple

250g (9oz) wholemeal flour or rye flour

20g (¾oz) baker's yeast, crumbled or 10g dried

575g (1lb 4¼oz) caster sugar

250g (9oz) dried figs, roughly chopped

250g (9oz) sultanas

125g (4½oz) mixed chopped candied peel with dried cherries, plus extra to decorate

60g (2¼oz) hazelnuts or walnuts, roughly chopped

60g (2¼oz) ground almonds

½ tbsp ground cinnamon

½ tsp ground star anise

Methodology

1. The day before you plan to bake the cake, place the dried pears and apples in a large bowl, cover with plenty of cold water and soak overnight.

2. The next day, drain the fruit, reserving all the liquid. Place 175ml (6fl oz) of the reserved liquid in a small saucepan and heat gently until tepid.

3. Place the flour and yeast in a large bowl and pour in the warmed juice. Mix little by little until the dough begins to come together. Continue to stir and knead until you have a soft, sticky dough. Form the dough into a ball, cover with a cloth and leave to rise for 1 hour.

4. Meanwhile, roughly chop the soaked pears and apples and place in a large bowl with 375g (13oz) of the caster sugar, the remaining fruits, nuts, ground almonds, spices and kirsch. Stir well until combined, then set aside.

5. Once the dough has risen, carefully work the dough into the fruit and spices mixture using your hands. There will appear to be too little dough, but keep stirring and kneading until the fruits and

a little freshly grated nutmeg

a pinch of ground cloves

a pinch of freshly ground pepper

50ml (2fl oz) kirsch

nuts are evenly dispersed. You will end up with a mixture that looks a little bit like chunky fruit mince or raw cake mix.

6. Preheat the oven to 180°C/Fan 160°C/350°F. Line your chosen tin(s) (either 12 × 125ml / 4fl oz individual loaf tins or 1 × 900g / 2lb loaf tin) with baking paper.

7. Put your dough into your chosen tin(s) between the tins, making sure you press it down well into the base and sides. Decorate by placing candied fruit along the length of the cake(s). Transfer to a baking tray and bake for 45–50 minutes if one cake or 40-45 minutes if individual until the cakes are a lovely golden brown.

8. Meanwhile, make a syrup. Put the remaining 200g (7oz) of sugar in a saucepan with 100ml (3½fl oz) of the remaining soaking liquid. Place over a low heat and stir until the sugar is dissolved, then bring to the boil and simmer for 1 minute.

9. Remove the cakes from the oven and leave to cool in the tin(s) for 5 minutes, then lift out and transfer to a wire rack. Immediately drizzle the cake(s) with the fruit syrup, then leave to cool completely on the wire rack.

Conversions

Below are the main conversions for both metric and imperial units.

WEIGHT CONVERSIONS

Grams	Ounces
10g	¼oz
15g	½oz
20g	¾oz
30g	1oz
40g	1½oz
50g	1¾oz
60g	2¼oz
70g	2½oz
80g	2¾oz
90g	3¼oz
100g	3½oz
150g	5½oz
200g	7oz
250g	9oz
300g	10½oz
350g	12oz
400g	14oz
450g	1lb
500g	1lb 2oz

VOLUME CONVERSIONS

Millilitres	Fluid Ounces
50ml	2fl oz
80ml	2¾fl oz
100ml	3½fl oz
125ml	4fl oz
150ml	5¼fl oz
175ml	6fl oz
200ml	7fl oz
225ml	8fl oz
250ml	9fl oz
275ml	9½fl oz
300ml	10½fl oz
350ml	12fl oz
400ml	14fl oz
500ml	18fl oz
750ml	26½fl oz
1 litre	35fl oz

LIQUIDS

Spoons & Cups	Millilitres
½ teaspoon	2.5ml
1 teaspoon	5ml
1 tablespoon	15ml
¼ cup	60ml
⅓ cup	80ml
½ cup	125ml
1 cup	250ml

Index

Dedication:

To Arthur and Dorothy,

Thank you for being our inspiration. We see the world
through your eyes and every day you make us proud as
we watch you living life to the full, absorbing every
experience and cherishing each new challenge. We simply
love sharing time with you both, being creative in the
garden sowing and planting, or in the kitchen cooking
and turning meals into celebrations. It gives us such
pleasure to see you thriving as you share with us the joys
of family life. We are in awe of the magic you sprinkle
over our lives and others. You are both so loved.

Your gushy mummy and daddy
XXX

Thank You

From the time before we had the idea of living in France, indeed, even before
we met and fell in love, there have been special people who have been in our lives
and given us both so much love and support that we can never repay or thank
them enough. We are blessed to have such loving family and friends and you
know just how much we love you.

Our work lives and personal lives are so incredibly entwined that the boundaries
are often blurred and actually don't really need to be defined. We have a very
special team supporting us at the chateau, in the UK and throughout the world
that is made up of the most amazing people. We rely on them all, and hopefully
we tell them regularly just how wonderful they are. Even when we are not
working together on a specific project, we still have them in our life
and as a family we feel lucky for that.

There is a final group of very important people that we are getting to know, and
that is those of you who have been following our adventure and have shown our
family such love and commitment. Many we have met and chatted to at events here
at the chateau, or in a shop or on the street in France, or Britain. Some we've met
after a show when we have been on tour, and there are many more we have yet to
meet, but who have sent us a letter, a gift, or emails of kindness and support.

From the entire Strawbridge family – thank you.